Enochian
World
of
Aleister
Crowley

GW00649246

Enochian World
of
Aleister Crowley

Enochian Sex Magick

By
Aleister Crowley
Lon Milo Duquette
Christopher S. Hyatt, Ph.D.

Sex Magick Symbols Illustrated By
David P. Wilson

NEW FALCON PUBLICATIONS
TEMPE, ARIZONA, U.S.A.

International Standard Book Number: 0-56184-029-7
Library of Congress Catalog Card Number: 91-60791

First Edition 1991
Second Printing 1993
Third Printing 1997
Fourth Printing 2002

The paper used in this publication meets the minimum requirements of the American National Standard for Permanence of Paper for Printed Library Materials
Z39.48-1984

Address all inquiries to:
NEW FALCON PUBLICATIONS
1739 East Broadway Road #1-277
Tempe, AZ 85282 U.S.A.
(or)
320 East Charleston Blvd., #204-286
Las Vegas, NV 89104 U.S.A.

website: http://www.newfalcon.com
email: info@newfalcon.com

DEDICATED

TO

MASTER THERION

CONSTANCE AND JEAN-PAUL
GARY AND CINDY

ACKNOWLEDGMENTS

The authors wish to express their thanks to Nicholas Tharcher for book design; to David P. Wilson for the execution of the Sex Magick Symbols; to S. Jason Black for cover design; and to Gary Ford.

New Falcon would also like to express its thanks to David P. Wilson for the execution of the Sex Magick Symbols, which are based on designs by Mr. Duquette. The captions below the Sex Magick Symbols are the creation of Dr. Hyatt and Mr. Duquette.

TABLE OF CONTENTS

Foreword

By Christopher S. Hyatt, Ph.D.

How do you know when you are really beginning to understand a subject?

When you come to the realization that it is basically much easier than you ever imagined.

For years I avoided an in-depth study of Enochian Magick, believing it to be not only too ponderous a task but also anachronistically irrelevant. I considered it a quaint dead-end of Elizabethan magic, elements of which have trickled down the centuries and lodged themselves in modern ceremonial magick.

I admit that I had a certain level of curiosity and fascination, especially when I saw the painted tablets and Enochian "chess" equipment that Israel Regardie would display on rare occasions to his friends. But the idea of actually taking the time to make sense of this collection of complex and fragmentary material was totally intimidating. And the thought of having to learn an "angelic language" did not thrill me at all. I was quite happy to file Enochian Magick in the same drawer of my mind where I keep "*Secrets of Aztec Cardiology*" and "*Cooking with Barbed Wire.*" Then several years ago I was pleasantly disabused.

I had asked Crowley expert, Lon DuQuette, to write an epilogue for my book, *Secrets of Western Tantra,* (Falcon Press, 1989) and in the course of our discussion he asked me if I had ever utilized Enochian Angels for operations of Sex Magick. He was genuinely amused when I revealed my reasons for avoiding the subject and he suggested that if ever I wished to learn how to immediately perform Enochian Magick, I should simply read Crowley's **Liber Chanokh** and get started.

13

When I protested that I *had* read it, that in fact, it was included in *Gems From The Equinox,* (Falcon Press, 1982). He said, "then read it again, carefully, and this time assume that everything you need to know is right there in the text."

He continued. "It is much simpler than you think." He then encouraged me to call him if I ran into trouble.

His somewhat cavalier attitude was oddly reassuring, so I took some time that evening to reread *Chanokh.* I followed his advice and pretended it was the only book on the subject in the world. To my great surprise I discovered that everything seemed quite clear. Was this the same book that frustrated and confused me earlier? Did I all of a sudden become so much smarter? Questions that were raised by one sentence were answered in the next. The fundamentals of the system unfolded neatly before my eyes. In less than an hour, I felt perfectly competent to start basic operations. I had no reason to call Lon for advice.

When I did call him it was to tell him of my application of the system to elements of my Tantric practices and that I wished to publish *Chanokh* along with his comments and supplementary material of my own findings. I have enjoyed our collaboration very much for his enthusiasm for the subject has been irresistibly contagious. Now we invite you to enter *The Enochian World Of Aleister Crowley.*

Relax. It is much simpler than you think and I guarantee you that if you do embark upon the sexual practices all of your efforts will be well rewarded.

Introduction

By Lon Milo DuQuette

In the introduction of a recently published book on magick, the writer characterizes the Enochian material in Crowley's *Equinox* as being "scanty" and in "disarray". I am afraid I could not disagree more. In fact, it is so exquisitely comprehensive and laid out with such orderly neatness that, (to quote Masonic scholar, Gary Ford), "Crowley can only be criticized for being too anal retentive."

If the critic was capable of paying attention and spent the hour or less that it takes to read **Chanokh** she couldn't help but grasp the subject. This, in my opinion, cannot be said of any other text on the subject.

For example, the somewhat complex explanation of how the 18 Calls are ordered and combined for invocations of the 16 different subangles takes four pages in Regardie's *Complete Golden Dawn System Of Magic,* (Falcon Press, 1984). Crowley does it easily in *10 sentences.*

I will not argue that Crowley demands much from his readers. But in the case of **Liber LXXXIV vel Chanokh** the difficulty is that one finds it almost impossible to believe that so much is communicated in so few words.

> The genuineness of these Keys, altogether apart from any critical observation, is guaranteed by the fact that anyone with the smallest capacity for Magick finds that they work.
> Aleister Crowley

Twenty five years ago few members of the general occult community had ever heard of the

Enochian system of Magick. Those who were aware of its existence fell into two main categories:

I. Members of the surviving magical societies which operated in the basic traditions of **Ordo Templi Orientis, A∴A∴** or **The Golden Dawn**.

II. Individuals lucky enough to posses either of two long-out-of-print works:

The Equinox Volume I, Numbers 7 & 8
The Golden Dawn Volumes 1-4

The Equinox , Aleister Crowley's Magnum Opus, issued at six month intervals between 1909 and 1914, was the first modern publication to examine the Enochian system in the seventh and eighth books of the ten number series.

Israel Regardie's *Account Of The Teachings, Rites And Ceremonies Of The Golden Dawn* followed in four volumes, the first published in 1937 and the fourth in 1940.

Though material relating directly to Enochiana occupies only a fraction of the above texts, the quality of the material is unquestioned. Both provide clear, fundamental information that gives the student both a basic understanding of the system and all the tools necessary to begin to immediately apply it and operate Enochian Magick.

In 1969 Regardie's *Golden Dawn* was reissued in a two volume format and then in 1974 he edited and released *Gems From The Equinox* containing all the Enochian material from the original 10 volume set. Both works are still in print. *The Complete Golden Dawn System Of Magic,* (Falcon Press, 1984) Regardie's tour de force published shortly before his death, includes his invaluable, *Addendum to the Concourse of Forces.* This tome stands as a monument to both the man and the material. This time the Enochian Genii has stayed out of the bottle.

Since 1969 an increasing number of students have turned their attention to this attractive yet, at first glance, overwhelmingly complex system. Their diligence is rewarded with something very rare indeed—a magical system that really works!

This takes many arm-chair magicians entirely off guard. A legitimate encounter with an Elemental Spirit or an Angel of an Æthyr invariably leaves a more lasting impression on the magician than the phantoms of self-deluded wishful thinking that mark the "successful working" of the dilettante.

Today Enochiana commands a respectable amount of space on the shelves of your local occult or New-Age bookstore. Much of the original Dee material (still existent) has been reprinted and made available to an ever-growing body of readers. The students of the early 1970s have become the researchers and prolific authors of today.

Many of the new works are excellent and offer invaluable contributions to the ever-increasing library of Enochian knowledge. (The works of Robert Turner should be singled out for their insight and high level of scholarship.)

Some others I feel are of less value. While perhaps informative as examples of the "findings" of one magician's experimentation, the distinction is not always made clear as to what is the author's speculation and innovation and what actually are the procedures suggested in the original documents. Then, to make matters even more confusing, the author presumes to define to the reader what they can expect to experience, intimating that if they get anything else they are somehow in error.

In my opinion, these works are little more than guided meditations upon another magician's visions and deny the reader the challenge of self discovery and mastery. But I'm sure that new volumes such as these will continue to appear. I will not be surprised to someday see titles such as *The Enochian Cookbook*,or *I'm OK...You're Enochian* appearing at my local bookstore.

It is our aim to offer in a practical format, *Liber LXXXIV vel Chanokh,* Crowley's original presentation of basic Enochiana and make it *immediately* useful for the student who wishes to make use of it *now*.

This coupled with Regardie's fine Enochian Dictionary and pronunciation guide provides the reader with the minimum material necessary to get started. For the advanced student we offer practical instructions concerning *powerful **sexual** applications* of the system and the opportunity to re-evaluate the original information that the greatest magician of the 20th Century felt was most necessary to master first.

Chapter One

A Short, Brief History (Abridged)

*I have often read in thy [God's] books &
records, how Enoch injoyed thy favour &
conversation; with Moses thou was familiar;
And also that to Abraham, Issack & Jocob,
Joshua, Gideon, Esdras, Daniel, Tobias &
sundry others thy good angels were sent by thy
disposition, to Instruct them, informe them,
helpe them, yea in worldly and domestick
affaires, yea and sometymes to satisfie their
desires, doubtes, and questions of thy Secrete:*
Dr. John Dee (Sloane MS. 3188)

For God's sake, tell me what to think.
Asheigh Brilliant

It is said that the Enochian System of Magick, as
practiced today, is the Child of Four Fathers; John
Dee, Edward Kelly, S.L. (MacGregor) Mathers and
Aleister Crowley. While this is a grossly inaccurate
oversimplification, (Dr. Rudd, Elias Ashmole, Wynn
Westcott and Israel Regardie might at least be called
midwives), it is basically true.

Through the efforts of the unbelievably mercurial
Elizabethan mathematician, Dr. John Dee and his
equally *unbelievable* "psychic" partner, Edward Kelly,
the raw material for the Enochian System was
"dictated" through a series of Angelic communications
that lasted from 1582 to 1589. Copious records were
kept, many which have survived to the present.

Ironically, once Dee and Kelly went through the
heroic efforts to get all this information, it is believed
they did not do a great deal with it. Miraculously,
much of the material survived the nearly 3 centuries to

come to the attention of S. L. (MacGregor) Mathers in the late 1880s.

(Note: Enochian fragments were even found in the famous cypher manuscripts whose discovery was instrumental in the creation of the Hermetic Order of the Golden Dawn.)

Mainly due to his inspired scholarship and impeccable logic, Dee's and Kelly's "raw" material was hammered into a comprehensive and workable system of ceremonial Magick. The two major branches of the system were then grafted to the Adeptus Minor curriculum of the Golden Dawn.

Aleister Crowley, who joined the Golden Dawn in 1898 and attained the Grade of Adeptus Minor in 1900, was of course exposed to the Order's Enochian teachings. However, Crowley took the Enochian "ball" and ran with it farther than the founders of the Golden Dawn had ever dreamed possible.

His exploration of the 30 Æthyrs as chronicled in *The Vision And The Voice (Gems From The Equinox*, Falcon Press 1982) has been seriously compared to the visionary works of William Blake and the Qabalistic images of Ezekiel and the Revelation of Saint John the Divine.

It was also Aleister Crowley who reorganized and elucidated upon the Golden Dawn Enochian material and published it in *Equinox Vol. I, Nos. VII* and *VIII* as *A Brief Abstract Of The Symbolic Representation Of The Universe Derived By Doctor John Dee Through The Skrying Of Sir Edward Kelly.* (Subsequently and mercifully renamed *Liber LXXXIV vel Chanokh.*)

Chapter Two

Before We Start
Let's Get Something Straight

The student who waits to master the subject before proceeding to perform Magick, will never master the subject nor proceed to perform Magick or for that matter anything else. **Christopher S. Hyatt, Ph.D.**

Anyone who refuses to begin a magical operation because of fear of the "evil" forces that might be unleashed if he or she makes a mistake, has already made a mistake that has invoked a far greater "evil". **David P. Wilson**

Resign yourself at the outset to take responsibility for your own magical reality. When you have firmly assumed this responsibility you will realize that there is no Enochian universe per se. There is only *your* universe which you can access by the Enochian formulae. There is no Enochian magick per se. There is only *your* magick, facilitated by the methods of the Enochian system.

This is not to argue the concept of spirits and angels having a certain objective reality. Indeed, the fundamental operating principal of evocation is to give outward substance to inner realities. But the sooner you rid yourself of preconceived ideas of how all this is going to manifest the sooner you will be able to recognize it when it really *does* start to manifest.

For example, let us compare the Enochian system of Dr. Dee to a more familiar "system" of another Elizabethan genius.

The sensitive theater-goer reaps a rich harvest of intellectual and spiritual rewards whenever he or she sees a play by William Shakespeare.

21

Each character in the play, hero or villain, speaks the "truth" from their particular perspective and it is up to us as the audience, to analyze these "truths" and apply them toward understanding our own lives.

Restated in Magickal Language: *Each Angel in the system, Divine or Demonic, declares their nature from their particular perspective and it is up to me as the magician, to analyze their communication and apply that knowledge to the understanding of the Great Work.*

These "truths" would be the same "truths" if the actors were dressed traditionally, or as cowboys or as space aliens. Granted, *you* might be distracted and miss the point of Hamlet's soliloquy if it were delivered by a giant amoeba, but a Biologist might find it most profound.

Just as no two people see and react to a play in exactly the same way, so too, no two magicians will have identical experiences in evocation.

Dare To Be Lazy

If you are truly interested in performing Enochian Magick there is more than enough information between the covers of this book to help you grasp the theory, build the equipment and perform the magick. In fact you are encouraged to do so.

By following the suggestions in the section that follows you will avoid many time-consuming mistakes that have traditionally plagued the Enochian student.

Supplementary to the text of *Chanokh,* I have provided comments to each of the major sections and have added additional diagrams in the Appendix. I strongly suggest that you read these and refer to the diagrams *while* you read *Chanokh.* You will save many hours of confusion and frustration if you will take this simple advice.

Also, pay special attention to the "Hints". They are put there to steer you clear of the "rocks" of Crowley's *thrifty* use of the English language (not to mention his downright omissions and a typo or two).

Make it easy on yourself. Dare to be lazy.

Chapter Three

The Ten Minute Overview

The two pillars of modern Enochian Magick, as outlined in *Liber Chanokh* (Chapter Five) are The Elemental Watch-towers (including the Tablet of Union) and the "World" of the 30 Æthyrs. The first is:

The Elemental Watch-Towers Of The Universe And The Tablet of Union

These are the Elemental Tablets (Plates III, IV, V, VI, VII and VIII) which are constructed with the purest Hermetic logic and lettered according to the diagrams of Dee and Kelly. These letters form the names of the Spirits of *Fire, Water, Air* and *Earth*.

These are the "Elementals" of literature, the Salamanders of Fire, the Undines of Water, the Sylphs of Air and the Gnomes of Earth.

Exactly what are the Elements and, more importantly, why would anyone want to call up an Elemental Being? Below is a portion of our book *The Way of the Secret Lover: Tantra, Tarot and the Holy Guardian Angel* (New Falcon Publications, 1991) which touches upon the subject of the Elements.

The ancients viewed the Elements as the building blocks of creation. They divided them into four broad categories which they called FIRE, WATER, AIR and EARTH.

Of course these are not the chemical elements which combine to form the material world around us. Nor are they literally Fire, Water, Air and Earth. They are, most simply put, the totality of all the forces, energies and qualities in the universe divided into four broad categories. These categories, by their natures, bear a poetical resemblance to Fire,

Water, Air and Earth. These qualities are the foundation of both galaxies and sub-atomic particles and the limitless diversity of creation is the result of the infinite number of ways these four Elements can be mixed, combined and recombined.

It is interesting to note that modern physics postulates four fundamental forces; the **Strong Force**, *the* **Electro-Magnetic Force**, *the* **Weak Force** *and the* **Gravitational Force** *that, by their characteristics, bear a remarkable resemblance to the ancient Elements:*

The ancients also postulated a Fifth Element (quite literally a "quintessence") which serves the double duty of binding the four Elements together and (at the same time) keeping them far enough apart to retain their individuality. This Fifth Element they called **SPIRIT.**

Once you have colored your Tablets you will see how the "Angels" of any given Element are formed, combined, mixed, recombined and reformed.

Obviously these Elementals are more than just the Salamanders in your fireplace, the sailor's Mermaid, Tinkerbell or Gimli the Dwarf. They have far more universal natures and as such are worthy of our attention. As a matter of fact they are at work, either efficiently or inefficiently, in each of us. Perhaps if we had a better understanding of our Elemental balance (or lack of it) we might get a clue as to how to improve our lives.

Note: What follows may seem a bit complicated to the new student. A full explanation of the operating procedure will be given in the following chapters.

For example, some years ago I accepted a job from an old friend who asked me to edit a psychology book he had just completed. I had never done such a thing before but I accepted with some hesitation.

26

The evening before I was to start I decided to invoke an Enochian Elemental Angel to help me put things in perspective and perhaps to give me a little boost on my first day. I chose to invoke **SOAIZNT** the Mercury Senior of the *Water* Tablet. (My reasoning was that Mercury is the force that is traditionally associated with writing and matters of the mind and Water is the element of reflection and empathy which I felt would be necessary for a task such as this.)

The invocation was simple enough. I had my Tablet of Union and Elemental Tablets sitting upon a table in the center of the room. After a routine Banishing Ritual of the Pentagram I opened the Temple in the Grade of 3°=8° as written in *Chanokh* then performed the Hexagram Ritual invoking Mercury (Planetary Seniors are invoked by the Hexagram) then I simply recited the *Fourth Call* straight out of *Chanokh*.

At first I "saw" nothing. (My skrying technique is to sit quietly with my eyes closed.) I felt somewhat stimulated and remember thinking that I should do this ritual whenever I needed to stay awake—when suddenly *it* was there. It had a basic humanoid form but it looked as if it had a "skin" made entirely of silver reflective material. Not stiff like a series of mirrors or facets, but smooth, almost liquid. Everywhere I looked on its "body" I saw myself reflected. It was breathtakingly beautiful. I was dumbfounded. After a moment when I could think straight again, I repeated the name, **SOAIZNT** (the standard procedure to test a vision.) It seemed to gain strength and become clearer with each repetition of its name so I felt confident that what was in front of me was indeed what I had called up. The question was now 'what am I going to do with this guy'? It took a little effort but I finally remembered the reason for the operation. I asked if it could help me to better understand another's thoughts and to efficiently transfer these thoughts to the written word. It indicated it could and produced a mirror upon which it drew a figure. I "felt" that I was to somehow use this figure as a tool to achieve my goal. I drew it on a piece of scratch paper and after the obligatory banishing I gazed upon it for a few minutes then went to bed. The next morning I decided I would take the figure **SOAIZNT** gave me and simply draw it at the top of each page of my daily note pad where I would be forced to look at it almost continually. Throughout the course of the project (which went surprisingly well by the way) I was focused upon this symbol and constantly reminded of the invocation and the incredible vision of the Angel who aids works of this nature.

In practical workings such as this it is very helpful to bring *something* from the vision back into *this* world.

In the *everyday* world of our waking consciousness life forms, such as people, animals, plants, etc., we perceive as living "beings." On the other hand, symbols such as triangles, pentagrams, letters, etc., we perceive as abstractions, springboards to a variety of ideas. In the "magical" world it is just the opposite. When we "see" a life form, such as an Angel or a unicorn or an aardvark, it is an abstract personification of an *idea*. Symbols, on the other hand, are "living beings" on that plane, the true life forms of the magical universe.

As you can imagine these symbol-life forms can be powerful tools in the hands of the magician. Bringing them through to our objective world is an important part of practical workings.

The second pillar is:

The Thirty Æthyrs Whose Dominion Extendeth In Ever-Widening Circles Beyond The Watch-Towers Of The Universe

These are the "heavens" or Aires of the system. Starting with the *30th* Æthyr and working to the *1st*, the magician explores only as far as his or her personal level of Initiation will permit. This process is comparable to "pathworkings" of the Qabalistic system. In Enochian terms, the "Great Work" of the magician is to master all 30 Æthyrs. (Starting with 30 and ending with 1)

Experiences with the 30 Æthyrs are highly personal and entirely unique to each magician. Working with the Æthyrs can be a lifetime endeavor and it is entirely presumptuous and inappropriate for another individual to "guide" another in this area.

Thus, with these two branches of the system, the Elemental and the Æthyric, we have formulae to access both the phenomenal world of the Elements and private world of our own Spiritual Journey.

Both types of operations require the ability on the part of the magician to skry or "travel in the Spirit Vision." If you are not already a talented skryer there is no better way to train than Enochian Magick, especially elemental workings.

There are as many skrying techniques as there are magicians who skry. Dee and Kelly gazed into a concave obsidian mirror. Crowley held a large topaz mounted upon a wooden cross to his forehead. But other methods include gazing into crystals, ink, fire or even a blank TV screen. You can sit in a chair or on the floor or lie on your back. You can close your eyes or keep them open. Use what works for you. As it is a subjective, (well, maybe not entirely subjective) experience, the choice is yours. I was amused to hear one skryer's abilities criticized for being done in a "light trance" state. We should all be so lucky!

For anyone who has tried unsuccessfully to skry in the past I offer the following hint.

Stop trying to skry!

Don't try to "see" a vision in your mind. The vision is already going on in the part of your mind (the right side of your brain) where you are not currently focused. (Don't criticize the movie if you go to the theater, buy a ticket then choose to stay in the lobby.) When you refocus your attention to that part of your mind you will find the "vision" in progress. It's impossible to refocus while you are consciously *trying* to refocus. So stop trying. Relax.

This change of focus happens each time you drop off to sleep. There is a moment when your thoughts begin to take visual form. You have a choice for a brief moment of "snapping out of it" or relaxing and "going with it, allowing yourself to change your focus for the rest of the night.

When you skry you are not asleep but neither are you focused on the objective world as analyzed by the left side of your brain. You relax and *allow* yourself to focus on the subjective, visual world of your brain's right hemisphere.

The most important thing to remember is not to project an objective reality to another skryer's vision. This is the flaw of "guided Pathworkings" or meditations upon another magician's visions. It is *your* magical universe you are dealing with and no one else's. (You are well advised to test your own visions and take them with a rather large grain of salt as well.)

Chapter Four

Comments On
Liber LXXXIV vel Chanokh

THE TITLE "LIBER LXXXIV"

The original title first published in *Equinox* Vol. I Nos. VII & VIII was *A Brief Abstract Of The Symbolic Representation Of The Universe Derived By Dr. John Dee Through The Skrying Of Sir Edward Kelly.*

LXXXIV (84) is the Qabalistic numeration for *Chanokh*, the Hebrew spelling of Enoch.

Note: When originally published the title did not bear the number. Crowley assigned the number 84 when the Syllabus of the Official Instructions of A∴A∴ was published in *The Blue Equinox*. Since then, due to a series of typographical errors, the number *LXXXIX* (89) has been mistakenly used in the title of published works. For our purposes we will refer to it simply as *Chanokh*.

PART I
THE HOLY TWELVEFOLD TABLE

The Holy Table is part of the "furniture" of the Temple and does not directly concern Elemental or Æthyrical workings. Angels found on the Holy Table are not called forth in these operations.

The original table top measured 35 7/8in X 36 1/4in X 7/10in.

Note: There is good reason to believe that the illustration as printed in *Chanokh*, (Plate I) is in error. Plate I is reproduced from Casaubon's *A True and Faithful Relation of what Passed for Many Years Between Dr. John Dee and Some Spirits...*published in 1659. It is now believed that, due to a 17th Century printer's error, Casaubon's version (and consequently everybody's since) was printed with the letters in reverse order. One of Dee's descriptions of the Table indicates it resembled the illustration we have included in the Appendix (Diagram A) of this book. This is regarded as the correct version. (Note: The Plates referred to are *not* in the Appendix but in the text of *Chanokh* itself [Chapter Five of this book]. All of the diagrams are in the Appendix of this book and are not original *Chanokh* illustrations.)

THE SEVEN TALISMANS

Like the Holy Table, these are considered Temple "furniture" and do not directly concern Elemental or Æthyrical workings. Spirits found on these talismans are not called forth in these operations.

The illustrations in Plate I are too small to read. Enlargements from the 17th Century manuscript, Dr. Rudd's Treatise, are included in the Appendix (Diagram B) of this book. It is interesting to note that the names on these "planetary" talismans are those of the Goetia. This indicates (or at least implies) Dee's familiarity with the LEMEGETON and his attempt, at least early in his workings, to incorporate it in the Enochian system.

PART II
THE HOLY SEVENFOLD TABLE
THE SIGILLUM DEI ÆMETH

Perhaps the most widely recognized diagram of the Enochian system, the Sigillum Dei Æmeth does not directly concern Elemental or Æthyrical workings. Like the Holy Table and the Talismans, its Angels are not called forth in these operations. Nevertheless it is an important piece of temple "furniture" for upon it rested the Shew-stone or the skrying mirror.

Made from bee's wax as described in *Chanokh*, the four smaller versions were placed under the feet of the Holy Table, presumably to insulate it from "earthy vibrations". The fifth and larger one (about 9 inches in diameter) covered with a red cloth, was placed on the Holy Table to support the Shew-stone.

Note: The illustration on Plate II was taken from Dee's diaries. The large wax version on display at the British Museum is slightly different. For example on the actual wax version, there are 7 crosses on each of the 7 bars making up the main heptagram. The illustration shows only three bars with 7 crosses the other 4 containing only 3.

Even though the above items of temple furniture are unnecessary for Elemental operations and for exploring the 30 Æthyrs, the reader might like to make his or her own versions of them to support the skrying mirror. Many of my (Dare to be lazy) students have simply made photographic enlargements of the illustrations that appear in this book and have mounted them on wood or foam board.

PART III

This is the most important section for the student to grasp. It deals directly with the two branches of the system of the most practical value, *The Elemental Tablets and the Tablet of Union* (sometimes referred to as the Black Cross.) and the *30 Æthyrs* or Aires. By using the information in this section the serious student will eventually construct the fabled equipment of the art.

This is also where many become confused and discouraged. Admittedly it will take the reader's full attention to wade through this section. This is not because Crowley is being deliberately obscure. On the contrary, it is because he is being almost unbelievably economical with his choice of words and the ordering of his thoughts.

I hope the following hints will save you some difficult moments.

HINT # 1
BE PREPARED FOR INCONSISTENCES
IN THE LETTERING OF THE TABLETS

Don't panic when you discover alternate spellings to names drawn from the Elemental tablets. This is due to the fact that Dee and Kelly (at the direction of the communicating angels) made several revisions to the tablets. To help you, we have included in the Appendix charts showing alternate and multiple lettering (See Diagram E).

HINT # 2
CAREFULLY READ AND REFER
OFTEN TO THE PLATES

A picture is worth a thousand words and in this case many hours. To be able to see what Crowley is writing about will save you much valuable time. Plates IV, V, VI, VII & VIII are lettered in Enochian. For English equivalents refer to the Appendix (assorted diagrams).

HINT # 3
REMEMBER, THE SAME GENERAL LAWS APPLY
TO ALL FOUR ELEMENTAL TABLETS.
TO UNDERSTAND ONE IS TO UNDERSTAND THEM ALL

For example; Crowley explains the Hierarchy of the *Three Holy Names*, the *Great Elemental King,* the *Six Seniors*, the *Two Divine Names of the Calvary Cross*, the *Kerubim* and the *Sixteen Lesser Angels* by using the Water Tablet (Plate V) as the example. The Hierarchy of the Fire, Air, and Earth Tablets are determined in exactly the same way.

Note: To make this section easier to understand, I have included in the Appendix (Diagram D) an English version of the *Water* Tablet conveniently split apart for easy viewing. If you keep this diagram in front of you while reading Part III of *Chanokh* I think you will have no trouble understanding what is being said.

BASIC TERMS

The Four Great Watch-Towers are often referred to as the Elemental Tablets of Air, Water, Earth and Fire.

Plate III shows them together; *Air* in the upper left-hand quarter, *Water* in the upper-right hand quarter, *Earth* in the lower left-hand quarter and *Fire* in the lower right-hand quarter.

Plates IV, V, VI, & VII show them singularly. Each of the Elemental Tablets is also divided into four sections by the two central vertical columns and the central horizontal line. (The *Linea Patris*, the *Linea Filii* and the *Linea Spiritus Sancti* respectively) This is also referred to as the Great Central Cross of the Elemental Tablet. (See Diagram D).

The four sections of the Elemental Tablet created by the Great Central Cross are called Subangles which are also attributed to the four Elements. (*Air* in the upper left-hand quarter, *Water* in the upper-right hand quarter, *Earth* in the lower left-hand quarter and *Fire* in the lower right-hand quarter.

In Diagram D in the Appendix of this book, you will see an example of the Water Tablet divided by the Great Central Cross and broken into its Subangles. (*Air of Water* in the upper left, *Water of Water* in the upper right, *Earth of Water* in the lower left, and *Fire of Water* in the lower right) Subangles on the *Air, Fire* and *Earth* Tablets are arranged in *exactly the same way.*

1. THE THREE HOLY NAMES OF GOD

(See Diagram D) The Three Holy Names of God are made up of the first three letters, the next four letters and the last five letters of the *Linea Spirtus Sancti* (the central horizontal line of each Elemental Tablet) For our example, the *Water* Tablet, the Three Holy Names are: **MPH ARSL GAIOL.**

Note: Don't let these names intimidate you. Just locate them. Don't worry about pronouncing them now. There is an excellent pronunciation guide provided later in this book.

Now try to locate The Three Holy Names on the Fire, Air and Earth Tablets.

2. THE GREAT ELEMENTAL KING

(See Diagram D) The eight letter Name of the Great Elemental King is formed by a clockwise whorl around the center of The Great Central Cross of the *Linea Patris*, the *Linea Filii* and the *Linea Spirtus Sancti*. The Great Elemental King may be considered the Sun Senior of the Tablet. The Great Elemental King of the *Water* Tablet is **RAAGIOSL.** Now try to locate the Great Elemental Kings on the other three Elemental Tablets.

3. THE SIX SENIORS

(See Diagram D) The 7 letter Names of the Six Planetary Seniors are also drawn from the Great Central Cross. Each Name starts in the middle of the Cross and moves towards the extremities. (Arrows in Diagram D show the directions the names are read and the Planet to which each of the Seniors is attributed). **This is the same for all four Elemental Tablets.**

In the case of the *Water* Tablet; **SAIINOV** is the Senior of Jupiter, **SOAIZNT** is the Senior of Mercury, **LAOAZRP** is the Senior of the Moon,

36

LIGDISA is the Senior of Saturn, **SLGAIOL** is the Senior of of Venus and **LSRAHPM** is the Senior of Mars. Now locate the Six Seniors on the three other Elemental Tablets.

4. THE CALVARY CROSSES

(See Diagram D) Each of the four Subangles on an Elemental Tablet contains a Calvary Cross. The two Angels of the Calvary Cross rule the Subangle. With the first Name (the vertical line — reading from top to bottom) you call forth the Power of the Subangle.

With the second Name (the horizontal line — reading from left to right) you compel the Power to obedience. (We will see how to do this later) These names as they apply to the *Water* Tablet appear in the text of *Chanokh*.

Remember, there are four Calvary Crosses in each Elemental Tablet. Now locate the four Calvary Crosses in the subangles of each of the four Elemental Tablets.

5. THE KERUBIM

(See Diagram D) The four letter Name of the Kerub is found above the arms of the Calvary Cross of each subangle. The letters of the Cross itself are never included in the Kerub's name.

The Kerub rules the *angels* who reside below the arms of the Cross. The four letters in the name of the Kerub can be rearranged in different orders to create different Kerubs who in turn rule different *angels* beneath the arms of the cross. (The letters of their names rearranged exactly as those of the rearranged Kerub.)

Note: A great deal of confusion exists concerning this statement in *Chanokh*:

They are ruled by names of God formed by prefixing the appropriate letter from the 'black cross' to their own [the Kerubim] names...There is disagreement among scholars as to which letters from the "Black Cross" (the Tablet of Union) are "appropriate." If you refer to Diagram G you will see that 16 of the 20 squares correspond to the 16 subangles of the four Elemental tablets.

The most popular theory maintains that these are the appropriate letters to help form the name of the "God" that rules the Kerub of any given Subangle. Let us use the example of the Elemental Tablet of Water (Diagram D) the Kerub of the Subangle of Fire is **NLRX.** Now refer to Diagram G and find the Fire of Water square. It is the fifth square of the second line. "**A**" (The "**A**" in HCOMA). So the God that rules **NLRX** would be **ANLRX.**

Please remember that there is disagreement, even among very knowledgeable experts, about these "God" names and where exactly they fit in the Enochian Hierarchy.

I advise beginning students to first become adequately fluent in basic hierarchical workings then develop for themselves a structure for these "supercharged" angels. The system does not pivot on this point.

6. THE FOUR MIGHTY AND BENEVOLENT ANGELS

(See Diagram D) These **Angels** are found beneath the horizontal bar of the Calvary Cross and are last in the Hierarchy of the Elemental Angels. They are extremely interesting and can provide great insight into the nature of the Elements. (Again, the names are only of four letters).

Note: Remember these four Angels are ruled by their Kerub who is found above the horizontal arm of the Calvary Cross. When you make a different Kerub (by changing the order of the letters in its name) you automatically make four new sets of Angel names beneath the arm of the Calvary Cross (by changing the

order of the letters of their names in the same manner
as the new Kerub.)

7. THE DEMONS OR ELEMENTALS

(See Diagram D) Unfortunately the definitive
instructions promised by Crowley were not
forthcoming and experts and students alike are left to
speculate and disagree. The reader is encouraged to
join in this quest. It is clear that they are not routinely
called forth in workings of the Elemental Tablets.

[Following Crowley's comments on the Triliteral
names of demons (above) he begins a second section
of PART III with subheadings 1-5.]

PART III
(SECOND SECTION)

As you can see from Plates IV, V, VI, VII and
VIII, the Squares of the Elemental Tablets and the
Tablet of Union are really Pyramids with flat tops. The
Pyramid with its four sides and top is an especially
appropriate symbol for the Four Elements ruled by
Spirit. Each side of an Enochian Pyramid has a very
specific attribute.

There are 20 Pyramids in the Tablet of Union and
156 in each of the four Elemental tablets. Each
Pyramid houses an Angel with a one letter name. The
attributes of that Angel are determined by the
positioning of the Pyramid upon the Tablet and
proportions of the different Elements represented on its
four sides. When two Pyramids are combined they
form an Angel with a two letter name whose attributes
are a bit more complex. And so on.

To most easily understand how these attributes
are determined I will give the reader *the most valuable
hint of all:*

HINT # 4.
HAND COLOR PLATES
IV, V, VI, VII, & VIII

Before attempting to understand the second section of Part III, you are well advised to make photocopies of Plates IV, V, VI, VII & VIII and then hand color the Pyramids. By coloring the Pyramids you will learn, in the fastest and easiest way possible, the logic behind their construction.

THE COLORING KEY FOR EACH PYRAMID

Leave the center square of each Pyramid (which contains the letter) uncolored for the time being.

Sides with the *Spirit* Symbol	✳	White
Sides with the *Fire* Symbol	△	Red
Sides with the *Water* Symbol	▽	Blue
Sides with the *Air* Symbol	▲	Yellow
Sides with the *Earth* Symbol	▼	Green or Black

I suggest you start with the Tablet Of Union, (Plate VIII or the English lettered version in the Appendix, Diagram G).

Even though it is small, it is a very important Tablet for its Angels, **EXARP, HCOMA, NANTA & BITOM,** rule the other four Elemental Tablets, (**EXARP** rules the *Air* Tablet, **HCOMA** rules the *Water* Tablet, **NANTA** rules the *Earth* Tablet and **BITOM** rules the *Fire* Tablet.)

The Tablet Of Union is considered the Elemental Tablet of *Spirit*. The four Elements are represented in their purest form, undifferentiated by the level of admixture that characterizes the other four Elemental Tablets.

The Tablet Of Union acts in exactly the same manner as Spirit acts upon the four Elements. It binds them together so they can combine to be the building blocks of creation *yet* keeps them separated just enough to prevent the loss of their individual and fundamental natures. This active and passive quality of Spirit is the reason that there are *two* types of Spirit Pentagrams, Active and Passive.

The Angels of the Tablet Of Union can be said to be the very "roots" of the Angels of the Elemental Tablets.

Once you have colored your Tablet Of Union, you will discover that a very simple pattern is formed by the attributes in the Lines and Files (or Columns). The top and bottom section of each Pyramid is attributed to Spirit. The right side is attributed to the Primary Element (as dictated by which *Line* the Pyramid is located) and the left side is attributed to the Secondary Element (as dictated by which *Column* it is located).

Note: This and what follows below will be laughably easy to understand if you have taken *five minutes* and colored your Tablet Of Union.

THE LINES

The four five letter Names (**EXARP, HCOMA, NANTA** and **BITOM**) are the Primary Spirits of the Elements. Each Spirit governs an entire Elemental Tablet.

EXARP is the Spirit of Air and governs the entire Air Tablet. The right section of each Pyramid of **EXARP** is Air.

HCOMA is the Spirit of Water and governs the entire Water Tablet. The right section of each Pyramid of **HCOMA** is Water.

NANTA is the Spirit of Earth and governs the entire Earth Tablet. The right section of each Pyramid of **NANTA** is Earth.

BITOM is the Spirit of Fire and governs the entire Fire Tablet. The right section of each Pyramid of **BITOM** is Fire.

THE COLUMNS

This same order of Air, Water, Earth and Fire is repeated in the Columns of the Tablet Of Union as Secondary attributions which appear on the left section of each Pyramid. (See Diagram G)

The first Column, **EHNB** is the purest of all the Column Names.

Each letter rules its respective Line and is three parts Spirit and one part its respective Element.

> **E** governs **EXARP**
> **H** governs **HCOMA**
> **N** governs **NANTA**
> **B** governs **BITOM.**

The sixteen letters of the remaining four columns contain both Primary and Secondary attributions. (Remember, the Secondary attribution is located upon the left section of these Pyramids.) These sixteen letters govern the sixteen Subangles of the Elemental Tablets.

X = Air of Air	**A** = Water of Air
C = Air of Water	**O** = Water of Water
A = Air of Earth	**N** = Water of Earth
I = Air of Fire	**T** = Water of Fire

R = Earth of Air	**P** = Fire of Air
M = Earth of Water	**A** = Fire of Water
T = Earth of Earth	**A** = Fire of Earth
O = Earth of Fire	**M** = Fire of Fire

An easy way to think about how the Tablet Of Union relates to the other four Tablets is to pretend you have an "Elemental Microscope".

Take the letter **E** from **EXARP** and put it under your microscope. You will see the entire **Air** Elemental Tablet.

Take the letter **O** from **BITOM** and put it under your microscope. You will see the *Earth* Subangle of the Tablet of *Fire*.

Take the second letter **N** from **NANTA** and put it under your microscope. Your will see the *Water* Subangle of the *Earth* Tablet, etc.

After you have colored your Tablet Of Union color each of the four Elemental Tablets. (You may purchase all of these beautifully mounted on boards from New Falcon Publications.)

HINT # 5
COLOR EACH ELEMENTAL TABLET
IN FOUR STEPS

Note: There are various ways the Pyramids of the Great Central Cross may be colored. We have chosen the method below because the attributes are uniformly determined through Elemental rulerships.

STEP 1:
THE GREAT CENTRAL CROSS

The **Top** section of each Pyramid of the **Great Central Cross** represents **Spirit** and is painted White.

The *Bottom* section of each Pyramid of the Great Central Cross represents the Element of the Tablet. In the case of the *Water* Tablet it is painted Blue. (When painting the *Fire* Tablet the bottom sections of the Great Central Cross would be Red, the *Air* Tablet Yellow, the *Earth* Tablet, Green or Black)

The *Left* side of each Pyramid of the Great Central Cross represent the Signs of the Zodiac. These are grouped in threes by element and positioned as describe in *Chanokh*.

The *Fire* Signs (Aires, Leo and Sagittarius) are colored Red.

The *Water* Signs (Cancer, Scorpio and Pisces) are colored Blue.

The *Air* Signs (Libra, Aquarius and Gemini) are colored Yellow.

The *Earth* Signs (Capricorn, Taurus and Virgo) are colored Green (or Black)

The *Right* side of each Pyramid of the Great Central Cross represent the planetary rulership of the 36 decans of the Zodiac. There are 36 decans and 36 Pyramids in the Great Central Cross. For our purpose we color the planets according to the rulership of the fixed signs:

Saturn and Mercury for *Air* are colored Yellow
Jupiter and the Sun for *Fire* are colored Red
Venus and the Moon for *Earth* are colored Green
or (Black)
Mars for *Water* is colored Blue.

STEP 2:
THE CALVARY CROSSES

The *Top* section of each Pyramid of the Calvary Crosses of the subangles represents *Spirit* and is painted white.

The *Bottom* section of each Pyramid of the Calvary Crosses of the subangles represent one of the ten *Sephiroth* of the Qabalistic Tree of Life and are

numbered according to Plates IV, V, VI and VII. We
suggest for the time being, that you leave the Bottom
sections White and simply number them in black. Later
you may wish to paint them one of the four traditional
colors of the Sephiroth.

The *Left* section of each Pyramid of the Calvary
Crosses of the subangles represent the Element of the
Tablet. In the case of the *Water* Tablet, the Left section
of the Pyramids of each of the four Calvary Crosses
would be painted Blue.

The *Right* section of each Pyramid of the Calvary
Crosses of the subangles represent the Element of the
subangle itself and painted accordingly. [Upper Left-
hand subangle (Air-Yellow), Upper Right-hand
subangle (Water-Blue), Lower Left-hand subangle
(Earth-Green or Black), Lower Right-hand Subangle,
(Fire-Red)] This pattern is the same for all four
Elemental Tablets.

STEP 3:
THE KERUBIC ANGELS

These are found above the arms of the Calvary
Crosses.

The Top section of each of the four Kerubic
Pyramids represent the Elemental Tablet and are
colored accordingly. In the case of the Water Tablet,
blue.

The Bottom section of each of the four Kerubic
Pyramids represent the Element of the subangle itself
and is colored accordingly.

Color the *Right* and *Left* sections of each of the
four Kerubic Pyramids as indicated in Plates IV, V, VI
and VII. The order that the elements are arranged
follow a logical permutation and dictate the order of the
Lines and Columns of the 16 Lesser Pyramids found
below the arms of the Calvary Cross.

STEP 4:
THE SIXTEEN LESSER PYRAMIDS

These are found below the arms of the Calvary Crosses.

The *Left* section of each Pyramid of the Lesser Angels represents the Elemental Tablet. In the case of the *Water* Tablet it is colored Blue.

The *Right* section of each Pyramid of the Lesser Angels represents the subangle and is colored accordingly.

Color the *Top* and *Bottom* section of each of the sixteen Lesser Pyramids as indicated in Plates IV, V, VI. and VII. Notice how the coloring order is dictated by the squares of the Kerubic Angels.

Granted, all this may take a few hours to execute but it will save you months (or as in my case, years) of confusion.

Now with your colored Tablets before you, read the material in the Second section of Part III of *Chanokh* and marvel at the "method" to the "madness."

PART IV
THE ENOCHIAN ALPHABET
AND THE ENOCHIAN LANGUAGE

One of the most unique characteristics of Enochian Magick is that the invocations are recited in a language completely unique to the system.

This language comes down to us as the result of the workings of Dr. John Dee and Edward Kelly and, according to their records, was taught to them by the Enochian Angels themselves.

Israel Regardie in his massive work, *The Complete Golden Dawn System of Magic* (New Falcon Publications, 1984), makes the following comments:

The Enochian language is without any history prior to the skrying of Edward Kelly and John Dee. There is no record of its prior existence, regardless of some fanciful theories which have been invented to account for it. The Enochian language is not just a haphazard combination and compilation of divine and angelic names drawn from the Tablets. Apparently, it is a true language with a grammar and syntax of its own. Only a superficial study of the invocations suffice to indicate this to be a fact. The invocations are not strings of words and barbarous names, but are sentences which can be translated in a meaningful way and not merely transliterated.

I believe, when invoking, that it is of the utmost importance to recite the Call or Calls in Enochian and not use an English translation. Not that it is unimportant for the Magician to know exactly what is being said but it is obvious to me that the intelligences who delivered this language to Dee and Kelly did not do it to hear themselves talk.

Reciting in Enochian instantly changes one's consciousness and induces a state of mind conducive to magical working.

The Calls themselves are very unique and are nothing like the tedious beseechments and endless whining and self debasement that characterize Goetic evocations. Rather, in the Angel's native tongue, they *sing* of its attributes and environment and offer a dignified invitation to communicate with the Magician.

This format is irresistible to the Angel. Think about it. If a mouse crawled up on your shoe and started to squeak, you would only give it as much attention as you would need to chase it away. But if it crawled up on your shoe, called you by name and then began to recite, in English, a litany of recognizable personal traits:

... Oh thou who art so huge, who wakest with the music of the clock-radio and who bringest

47

*in the morning paper, who with thy mouth
consumest the eggs of the hen and wipeth thy
lips with paper...*

... you would sit up and take notice. You might
even try to have a meaningful conversation with the
little fellow. You wouldn't even mind if he spoke with
a thick accent!

The Enochian Calls as they appear in *Chanokh* are
written phonetically and are very close to the standard
used by the Golden Dawn which appear in Regardie's
Enochian Dictionary in the Appendix of this book.

Plate IX shows the Enochian Alphabet and Plates
I, IV,V, VI, VII, VIII are lettered in Enochian.

PART V
THE THIRTY ÆTHYRS OR AIRES

As we will read in *Chanokh*, Crowley says that
Dee:

*...symbolized the Fourth-Dimensional Universe
in two dimensions as a square surrounded by 30
concentric circles (the 30 Æthyrs or Aires)
whose radii increase in a geometrical
proportion*

The "square" mentioned above is the Four
Elemental Tablets and the Tablet of Union. These are
quite literally Watch-Towers that stand at the very edge
of the phenomenal universe. Beyond the Watch-
Towers are the Æthyrs, the Aires, the Heavens. They
can be visualized as thirty spheres, one inside another
like layers of a glass onion. The Thirtieth, **TEX** is the
lowest and consequently the closest to the Watch-
Towers.

LIL, the First, is the highest and represents the
Supreme Attainment. It is the Great work of the
Magician to "explore" the Æthyrs one at a time, and
learn the lessons, master the problems and receive the
wisdom each has to offer.

Most anyone who cares to try has some level of success in the lower Æthyrs. It is most important to keep a detailed record of all workings because eventually you will reach a point beyond which you cannot pass. This point marks the limits of your present level of "initiation" and the last Æthyr you *could* successfully penetrate holds the key to your spiritual advancement.

Each of the Thirty Æthyrs is populated by Governors whose responsibilities are partially described in Dee's *Liber Scientiæ, Auxilii, et Victoriæ Terrestris*. For our purpose we will view the Governors as angelic personifications of the different facets of the Æthyrs. They serve as our guides and most importantly they are "someone" to whom we can talk and ask questions. The names of the each of the Thirty Æthyrs and their Governors is provided in the text of *Chanokh*.

Each Æthyr has three Governors (except the Thirtieth which has four). Sigils (signatures) of the Governors are taken from the Elemental Tablets showing that the influence of the Æthyrs is universal reaching even into the Watch-Towers of the Elements.

These sigils of the Governors are illustrated in Plate X and more clearly in Diagram F and are numbered 1 through 91. In order to more easily find the Sigil of each Governor, the reader is encouraged to number the list of Governors as found in Part V of *Chanokh* starting with **OCCODON-1, PASCOMB-2, VALGARS-3, DOAGNIS-4,** etc.

Ironically very little effort is required to "work" with the Æthyrs. One Call only is necessary for all thirty of them. The name of the Æthyr itself being the only variable.

Once the Call is recited the names of the Governors are vibrated one at a time. Often the vision changes drastically when the next Governor's name is vibrated. Take your time with each one and, as always, keep a detailed record of your operation.

Now let us turn our attention to the section of *Chanokh* designated in the text as:

PART II
THE FORTY-EIGHT CALLS OR KEYS

The calls or Keys activate the tablets and subangles in the same way as the power switch turns on a TV before selecting a channel.

At the beginning of this section Crowley tells us which Calls are used in all the various invocations of the Elemental system. He does so in the fewest words humanly possible. Perhaps the reader will appreciate the elucidation below.

FIRST KEY

Use first in all invocations of any of the Angels of the Tablet of Union. (It is not used in the invocation of any of the Angels of the Elemental Tablets.)

SECOND KEY

Use second as invocation of the Angels of the letters **E H N B** of the Tablet of Union. Like the FIRST CALL it is never used in the invocation of the Angels of the four Elemental Tablets. (The sequence of Calls being 1 and 2.)

Note: The Third, Fourth, Fifth and Sixth Keys are used in certain invocations of the Tablet of Union *and* in the Invocations of the Elemental Tablets. What follows immediately is how they are used in invocations of the Tablet of Union.

THIRD KEY

For invocations of the Angels of the letters of the line **EXARP** the sequence of Calls is 1, 2 and 3.

FOURTH KEY

For invocations of the Angels of the letters of the line **HCOMA** the sequence of Calls is 1, 2 and 4.

FIFTH KEY

For invocations of the Angels of the letters of the line **NANTA** the sequence of Calls is 1, 2 and 5.

SIXTH KEY

For invocations of the Angels of the letters of the Line **BITOM** the sequence of Calls is 1, 2 and 6.

THE ELEMENTAL TABLETS

THIRD KEY AIR

Use first in all invocations of the Angels of the Tablet of Air. (When invoking a Senior or the Angels of subangle Air of Air it is the only call necessary.)

FOURTH KEY WATER

Use first in all invocations of the Angels of the Tablet of Water (When invoking a Senior or the Angels of subangle Water of Water it is the only call necessary.)

FIFTH KEY EARTH

Use first in all invocations of the Angels of the Tablet of Earth. (When invoking a Senior or the Angels of subangle Earth of Earth it is the only call necessary.)

SIXTH KEY FIRE

Use first in all invocations of the Angels of the Tablet of Fire. (When invoking a Senior or the Angels of subangle Fire of Fire it is the only call necessary.)

SEVENTH KEY
WATER SUBANGLE OF AIR TABLET

For invocations of the Angels of the Water subangle of the Air Tablet, the sequence of Calls is 3 and 7.

EIGHTH KEY
EARTH SUBANGLE OF AIR TABLET

For invocations of the Angels of the Earth subangle of the Air Tablet, the sequence of Calls is 3 and 8.

NINTH KEY
FIRE SUBANGLE OF AIR TABLET

For invocations of the Angels of the Fire subangle of the Air Tablet, the sequence of Calls is 3 and 9.

TENTH KEY
AIR SUBANGLE OF WATER TABLET

For invocations of the Angels of the Air subangle of the Water Tablet, the sequence of Calls is 4 and 10.

ELEVENTH KEY
EARTH SUBANGLE OF WATER TABLET

For invocations of the Angels of the Earth subangle of the Water Tablet, the sequence of Calls is 4 and 11.

TWELFTH KEY
FIRE SUBANGLE OF WATER TABLET

For invocations of the Angels of the Fire subangle of the Water Tablet, the sequence of Calls is 4 and 12.

THIRTEENTH KEY
AIR SUBANGLE OF EARTH TABLET

For invocations of the Angels of the Air subangle of the Earth Tablet, the sequence of Calls is 5 and 13.

FOURTEENTH KEY
WATER SUBANGLE OF EARTH TABLET

For invocations of the Angels of the Water subangle of the Earth Tablet, the sequence of Calls is 5 and 14.

FIFTEENTH KEY
FIRE SUBANGLE OF EARTH TABLET

For invocations of the Angels of the Fire subangle of the Earth Tablet, the sequence of Calls is 5 and 15.

SIXTEENTH KEY
AIR SUBANGLE OF FIRE TABLET

For invocations of the Angels of the Air subangle of the Fire Tablet, the sequence of Calls is 6 and 16.

SEVENTEENTH KEY
WATER SUBANGLE OF FIRE TABLET

For invocations of the Angels of the Water subangle of the Fire Tablet, the sequence of Calls is 6 and 17.

EIGHTEENTH KEY
EARTH SUBANGLE OF FIRE TABLET

For invocations of the Angels of the Earth subangle of the Fire Tablet, the sequence of Calls is 6 and 18.

THE CALL OR KEY
OF THE THIRTY ÆTHYRS

As we have mentioned above, the Nineteenth Call, or Key of the Thirty Æthyrs, is the only call necessary for workings with the Æthyrs. It is only necessary to change the name of the Æthyr itself near the beginning of the Call.

Note: In a footnote in *Chanokh*, Crowley mentions a second name in the Call that "*...may appropriately be varied with the Aire*". Try as I may to discover a logical correlation between **LIL** (the Æthyr in question) and **IDOIGO** (the footnoted name in question), I cannot. Until I do, I will continue to vary the Call of the Thirty Æthyrs only with the name of the Æthyr itself. If I am wrong I am willing to be forgiven.

MINIMUM RECOMMENDED
OPERATING PROCEDURES

The question now arises "How do I go about implementing the above information to invoke the Angels of the Elemental Tablets or begin my exploration of the Æthyrs?"

The nature of the original Dee material is such as to make exact and definitive operating procedures unclear. In other books of Enochian Magick, particularly those written in the last 10 years, you will find elaborate instructions that differ considerably from what is suggested below.

As you become more familiar with the system you will develop your own sense of what is logical and appropriate. It is very important during the period of your learning curve to stay focused on *source* material such as *Chanokh*.

Chanokh provides basic operating instructions, though not always clearly. It is obvious that Crowley assumed the reader would have a basic magical education and would be able to proceed somewhat on their own understanding. These comments and the supplementary material in the Appendix are intended to help on both these fronts. But we should not ignore the obvious fact that Crowley's original presentation was very short and straightforward. Nowhere does he even hint that the Magician must engage in a long series of beseechments, coercions and just plain magical whinings that characterize other branches of magick.

What is unique about Enochian Magick is the absence of such infantile nonsense. Calls are addressed in the language of the beings involved. There is a simple hierarchy that needs to be recognized. The rest is between you and the Angels.

To make matters even simpler he provides us with five flawlessly constructed "Temple Openings" which are inserted prior to the First, Third, Fourth, Fifth and Sixth Keys. By performing the "Temple Openings" prior to reciting the Calls you will find almost half your work done. If you are unclear as to the appropriate signs, pentagrams or hexagrams used in the Temple Openings refer to the Appendix.

The simple procedure outlined below will take you anywhere you wish to go with the system. Of course you are free to expand and innovate upon the system as much as you feel necessary. (I would not, however, advise that you *omit* any of the following steps)

PRELIMINARY CONSIDERATIONS

TEMPLE ARRANGEMENTS

These can be as simple or as elaborate as you wish. A clean, uncluttered room with an altar or table in the center is perfectly adequate. You may wish to place your Elemental Tablets on the walls of the four quarters (*Air* in the East, *Fire* in the South, *Water* in the West, and *Earth* in the North) or you may wish to arrange them upon the altar. It is not essential to have any Tablets in the Temple at all.

DIRECTIONS OF THE WORKING

When invoking, that is when you wish to bring the Spirit to you, face the *micro*-cosmic-elemental direction dictated by the four winds; operations of *Air* in the East, *Fire* in the South, *Water* in the West and *Earth* in the North.

When you wish to visit the Spirit in its own world you face the *macro*-cosmic-elemental direction dictated by the Zodiac; operations of *Fire* in the East (Aries), *Earth* in the South (Capricorn), *Air* in the West (Libra) and *Water* in the North (Cancer).

For workings of the Thirty Æthyrs it does not matter which direction you are facing.

DETERMINE THE HIERARCHY
OF THE SPIRIT IN QUESTION

Remember the Temple Openings contain the invocations of the Three Holy Names of God and the Great Elemental King. *It is unnecessary for you to repeat these names in subsequent invocations.*

STEP ONE
PERFORM THE LESSER
BANISHING RITUAL OF THE PENTAGRAM

This is found in Chapter Seven. Any magical operation no matter how simple should be proceeded by a Lesser Banishing Ritual of the Pentagram.

STEP TWO
OPEN THE TEMPLE AND RECITE
THE APPROPRIATE CALL

Note: Remember, all Temple Openings are found in the text of Chanokh just prior to the appropriate Call.

EXAMPLE ONE

To invoke **EHNB** from the Tablet of Union:

1. Open the Temple with The Opening of the Portal of the Vault of the Adepts.

2. Recite The First Key and The Second Key.

3. Recite Enochian Conjuration (see below) inserting the Angel Name, **EHNB.**

EXAMPLE TWO

To invoke **EXARP** from the Tablet of Union:

1. *(Repeat 1 and 2 above.)* Open the Temple with The Opening of the Temple in the Grade of $2° = 9°$.

2. Recite The Third Key.

3. Recite Enochian Conjuration (see below) inserting the Angel Name, **EXARP.**

EXAMPLE THREE

To invoke the Keurbic Angel **TAAD** from the Air subangle of the Water Tablet:

1. Open the Temple with The Opening of the Temple in the Grade of $3° = 8^{\square}$.

2. Recite The Fourth Key (to open the Water Tablet).

3. Recite The Tenth Key (to open the Subangle of Air).

4. Recite Enochian Conjuration (see below) inserting the Angel Name, **TAAD**, the names of the six Seniors of the Water tablet: **SAIINOV, SOAIZNT, LAOAZRP, LIGDISA, SLGAIOL, LSRAHPM** and the Divine Names of the Calvary Cross, **OLGOTA** and **AALCO.**

EXAMPLE FOUR

To invoke the Lesser Angel **ACCA** from the Fire Subangle of the Air Tablet:

1. Open the Temple with The Opening of the Temple in the Grade of $2° = 9^{\square}$.

2. Recite The Third Key (to open the Air Tablet).

3. Recite The Ninth Key (to open the Subangle of Fire).

4. Recite Enochian Conjuration (see below) inserting the Angel Name, **ACCA**, the names of the six Seniors of the Air Tablet, **AAOXAIF, AVTOTAR, HTMORDA, HIPOTGA, AHAOZPI, HABIORO** and the Divine Names of the Calvary Cross, **AOURRZ** and **ALOAI** and Kerubic Ruler **XGZD.**

ENOCHIAN CONJURATION

The conjuration below was extracted from Crowley's Enochian translation of the First Conjuration of the Goetia. Simply insert the name of the Spirit you wish to work with and *any* and *all* the names of its hierarchial superiors.

IN ENOCHIAN

Ol vinu od zodakame, Ilasa, Gahe
(Insert Angel Name)
od elanusahe vaoresagi Iaida,
gohusa pujo ilasa, darebesa!
Do-o-i-ape____od____od____od____
od____(use as many names as necessary)
Ol vinu-ta od zodameta,
Ilasa, Gahe (Insert Angel Name)

IN ENGLISH

I invoke and move thee, O thou, Spirit _____
and being exalted above ye in the power of the
Most High, I say unto thee, obey!
In the name of __and__and __and __and ___
I do invoke and by invoking conjure thee, O
thou, Spirit _____.

Now set to work skrying. Keep paper and pencil handy. Some prefer to have a tape recorder running. It is important to maintain some level of objective consciousness. If you fall asleep you are likely to forget your vision and may run into unpleasant complications.

If you run into any "spiritual" characters that make you feel uncomfortable, test them first with the Holy Names from the Tablet you are working with or (in the case of the Thirty Æthyrs), the names of the Governors. If you are still having difficulties draw the appropriate banishing pentagram (see Appendix for Banishing Pentagrams) and withdraw from the vision.

Do not tire yourself. When you feel fatigued find an opportunity to withdraw from the vision and Banish.

STEP 3
CLOSE THE TEMPLE WITH THE
BANISHING RITUAL OF THE PENTAGRAM

I have found the Enochian system to be the safest, cleanest and most logical system of practical magick one can perform. But it is an art and as such requires not only study and practice but also inspiration and the love-hate relationship all artists have with their craft. It is my hope that our book has given you something to study, practice and inspire you.

Chapter Five

Liber LXXXIV vel Chanokh

A BRIEF ABSTRACT OF THE SYMBOLIC REPRESENTATION OF THE UNIVERSE DERIVED BY DOCTOR JOHN DEE THROUGH THE SKRYING OF SIR EDWARD KELLY

PART I

The Skryer obtained from certain Angels a series of seven talismans. These, grouped about the Holy Twelvefold Table, similarly obtained, were part of the furniture of the Holy Table, as shewn in Plate I.

Other appurtenances of this table will be described hereafter.

II

Other Pantacles were obtained in a similar manner. (Plate II) is the principal one, which, carved in wax, was placed upon the top of the table. On four others stood the feet of the table.

Note first the Holy Sevenfold Table containing seven Names of God which not even the Angels are able to pronounce.

$$\text{SAAI } \tfrac{21}{8} \text{ EME}$$
$$\text{BTZKASE}^{30}$$
$$\text{HEIDENE}$$
$$\text{DEIMOL}^{30}\text{A}$$
$$\text{I}^{26}\text{MEGCBE}$$
$$\text{ILAOI } \tfrac{21}{8} \text{ VN}$$
$$\text{IHRLAAL } \tfrac{21}{8}$$

These names are seen written without the heptagram within the heptagon.

By reading these obliquely are obtained names of Angels called—
(1) Filiæ Bonitatis or Filiolæ Lucis.
E, Me, Ese, Iana, Akele, Azdobn, Stimcul
(2) Filii Lucis.
I, Ih, Ilr, Dmal, Heeoa, Beigia, Stimcul
[These are given attributions to the Metals of the Planets in this order: Sol, Luna, Venus, Jupiter, Mars, Mercury, Saturn.]
(3) Filiæ Filiarum Lucis.
S, Ab, Ath, Ized, Ekiei, Madimi, Esemeli
(4) Filii Filiorum Lucis.
L (EL), Aw, Ave, Liba, Iocle, Hagone(l), Ilemese

See all these names in the heptagram of the great seal.

So also there are Seven Great Angels formed thus: take the corner letter S, then the diagonal next to it AB, then the next diagonal ATH, the the fourth diagonal, where is I with 21/8 (which indicates EL), and we have the name—

SABATHIEL

Continuing the process, we get: **ZEDEKIEL, MADIMIEL, SEMELIEL, NOGAHEL, CORABIEL, LEVANAEL.**

These names will be found in the Pentagram and about it.

These angels are the angels of the Seven Circles of Heaven.

These are but a few of the mysteries of this great seal: **SIGILLVM DEI ÆMETH**

III

The Shew-stone, a crystal which Dee alleged to have been brought to him by angels, was then placed upon this table, and the principal result of the ceremonial skrying of Sir Edward Kelly is the obtaining of the following diagrams, Plates III-VIII.

He symbolized the Fourth-Dimensional Universe in two dimensions as a square surrounded by 30 concentric circles (the 30 Æthyrs or Aires) whose radii increase in a geometrical proportion.

The sides of the square are the four great watch-towers (Plates IV-VII) which are attributed to the elements. There is also a "black cross" (or "central tablet" according to the arrangement shewn—compare the black cross bordering the tablets in Plate III with Plate VIII).

Plate III gives the general view.

[The reversed letters which form the word PARAOAN are written in Enochian for convenience, as our A and O are not distinguishable reverse from forward.]

Plate IV gives the complete attribution of the tablet of Air.

The 6th file is called Linea Patris.

The 7th file is called Linea Filii.

The 7th line is called Linea Spiritus Sancti.

The great cross divides the Tablet into four lesser (sub-elemental) Tablets, the left-hand top corner being Air of Air, the right-hand top corner Water of Air, the left-hand bottom corner Earth of Air, the remaining corner Fire of Air.

Each of these lesser Tablets contains a Calvary Cross of ten squares, which governs it.

Plates V, VI, and VII are similar for the other elements.

This is the way in which the names are drawn from the great Tablets. [Examples taken from Water Tablet.]

1. Linea Spiritus Sancti gives the Three Holy Names of God of 3, 4, and 5 letters respectively:

MPH ARSL GAIOL

2. A whorl around the centre of the Tablet gives the name of the Great Elemental King, **RAAGIOSL** [similarly for Air **BATAIVAH**, for Earth **ICZHHCAL**, for Fire **EDLPRNAA**].

3. The 3 lines of the central cross of Father, Son, and Holy Ghost give the names of 6 seniors. [Thus the 4 tablets hold 24 "elders," as stated in the Apocalypse.] They are drawn of seven letters, each from the centre to the sides of the tablet.

> Linea Patris, **SAIINOV** and **SOAIZNT**
> Linea Filii, **LAOAZRP** and **LIGDISA**
> Linea S.S, **SLGAIOL** and **LSRAHPM**

These three sets of names rule the whole tablet, and must be invoked before specializing in the lesser angles of the sub-elements.

4. The Calvary Crosses.

The name upon the cross read vertically is the name which calls forth the powers of the lesser angle.

> **NELAPR** (water of water)
> **OLGOTA** (air of water)
> **MALADI** (earth of water)
> **IAAASD** (fire of water)

The name read horizontally on the cross is that which compels the evoked force to obedience.

> **OMEBB** (water of water)
> **AALCO** (air of water)
> **OCAAD** (earth of water)
> **ATAPA** (fire of water)

5. Above the bar of the Calvary Cross remain in each case four squares. These are allotted to the Kerubim, who must next be invoked. They are:

> **TDIM**
> **DIMT**
> **IMTD**
> **MTDI,**

being metatheses of these four letters. The initial

determines the file governed; *e.g.,* **TDIM** governs the file which reads **T(o)ILVR**. These angels are most mighty and benevolent. They are ruled by names of God formed by prefixing the appropriate letter from the "black cross" to their own names.

6. Beneath the bar of the Calvary Cross remain 16 squares not yet accounted for. Here, beneath the presidency of the Kerubim, rule four mighty and benevolent angels—

    INGM
    LAOC
    VSSN
    RVOI

7. Triliteral names of demons or elementals are to be formed from these 16 squares, uniting the two letters on either side of the upright of the cross with a letter chosen from the Central Tablet or black cross in accordance with rules which will be given in their due place. Thus: **GM, IN, OC, LA** et cetera, form bases for these triliteral names.

The following rules explain how the sides of the pyramids of which the squares are formed are attributed to the Sephiroth, Planets, Elements, and Zodiacal signs.

1. Great Central Cross. This has 36 squares, for the decanates of the Zodiac.

On the left side of the Pyramid, Linea Patris has the Cardinal signs, the sign of the Element itself at the top, in the order of Tetragrammaton (Fire, Water, Air, Earth) going upwards.

Linea Filii has the Common signs in the same order.

Linea S.S. has the Kerubic signs, that of the element on the left, in the same order, right to left.

But the order of the decans in each sign is reverse, and thus the planets which fill the right-hand side of the Pyramids go in the first two cases downwards, and in the third from left to right.

The upper sides of the Pyramids are all attributed to the Element of Spirit, the lower sides to the Element of the Tablet.

Each square is also referred to the small card of the Tarot which corresponds to the Decan (refer to Crowley's work, *777*, Weiser, 1972).

2. Calvary Crosses.

Each has 10 squares.

The upper sides of the Pyramids are uniformly given to Spirit, the lower sides to the Sephiroth, in the order shewn. The left-hand sides are attributed to the element of the Tablet, the right-hand sides to the sub-element of the lesser angle.

3. Kerubic Squares.

The upper sides pertain to the element of the Tablet, the lower sides to the sub-element. Right and left-hand sides in this case correspond, according to a somewhat complex rule which it is unnecessary to give here. The attributions to the Court Cards of the Tarot naturally follow.

4. Lesser Squares.

The upper side of each pyramid is governed by the Kerub standing on the pile above it. The lower side is governed by the Kerub also, but in order descending as they are from right to left above. [See angle of Air of Water; the Kerubs go Earth, Fire, Water, Air (from the square marked D, the fifth from the left in the top rank of the Tablet), and downward the lower sides of the squares marked O, D, *E, Z (*this should probably read* O, D, X, Z. *Ed.*) go Earth, Fire, Water, Air.]

The left-hand side refers to the element of the Tablet, the right-hand side to the sub-element of the lesser angle.

5. The Black Cross of Central Tablet.

The upper and lower sides are equally attributed to Spirit.

The left-hand sides to the element of the file, in this order from left to right: Spirit, Air, Water, Earth, Fire.

The right-hand sides to the element of the rank in this order: Air, Water, Earth, Fire.

IV

Follows Plate IX, the Alphabet in which all this is written. It is the Alphabet of the Angelic Language. The invocations which we possess in that tongue follow in their due place.

[It is called also Enochian, as these angels claimed to be those which conversed with the "patriarch Enoch" of Jewish fable.]

V

The Thirty Æethyrs or Aires and their divisions and angels are as follows [We omit for the present consideration of the parts of the earth to which they are stated to correspond, and the question of the attributions to the cardinal points and the Tribes of Israel. These are duly tabulated in Dee's *Liber Scientiæ, Auxilii, et Victoriæ Terrestris*]:

Name of Aire	Names of Governor	Numbers of Servitors	In All
1. LIL.	OCCODON	7209	
	PASCOMB	2360	
	VALGARS	5362	14,931
2. ARN.	DOAGNIS	3636	
	PACASNA	2362	
	DIALIVA	8962	15,960
3. ZOM.	SAMAPHA	4400	
	VIROOLI	3660	
	ANDISPI	9236	17,296
4. PAZ.	THOTANF	2360	
	AXZIARG	3000	
	POTHNIR	6300	11,660

5. LIT.	LAZDIXI	8630	
	NOCAMAL	2306	
	TIARPAX	5802	16,736
6. MAZ.	SAXTOMP	3620	
	VAVAAMP	9200	
	ZIRZIRD	7220	20,040
7. DEO.	OBMACAS	6363	
	GENADOL	7706	
	ASPIAON	6320	20,389
8. ZID.	ZAMFRES	4362	
	TODNAON	7236	
	PRISTAC	2302	13,900
9. ZIP.	ODDIORG	9996	
	CRALPIR	3620	
	DOANZIN	4230	17,846
10. ZAX.	LEXARPH	8880	
	COMANAN	1230	
	TABITOM	1617	11,727

[Note that these 3 names come from the black cross, with the addition of an L. This L is one of the 8 reversed letters in the four watchtowers, the other seven forming the word **PARAOAN**, *q.v. infra.*]

11. ICH.	MOLPAND	3472	
	VANARDA	7236	
	PONODOL	5234	15,942
12. LOE.	TAPAMAL	2658	
	GEDOONS	7772	
	AMBRIAL	3391	13,821
13. ZIM.	GECAOND	8111	
	LAPARIN	3360	
	DOCEPAX	4213	15,684

14. VTA.	TEDOOND	2673	
	VIVIPOS	9236	
	OOANAMB	8230	20,139
15. OXO.	TAHANDO	1367	
	NOCIABI	1367	
	TASTOXO	1886	4,620
16. LEA.	COCARPT	9920	
	LANACON	9230	
	SOCHIAL	9240	28,390
17. TAN.	SIGMORF	7623	
	AYDROPT	7132	
	TOCARZI	2634	17,389
18. ZEN.	NABAOMI	2346	
	ZAFASAI	7689	
	YALPAMB	9276	19,311
19. POP.	TORZOXI	6236	
	ABAIOND	6732	
	OMAGRAP	2388	15,356
20. KHR.	ZILDRON	3626	
	PARZIBA	7629	
	TOTOCAN	3634	14,889
21. ASP.	CHIRSPA	5536	
	TOANTOM	5635	
	VIXPALG	5658	16,929
22. LIN.	OZIDAIA	2232	
	PARAOAN	2326	
	CALZIRG	2367	6,925
23. TOR.	RONOAMB	7320	
	ONIZIMP	7262	
	ZAXANIN	7333	21,915
24. NIA.	ORCAMIR	8200	
	CHIALPS	8360	
	SOAGEEL	8236	24,796

25. VTI.	MIRZIND	5632	
	OBUAORS	6333	
	RANGLAM	6236	18,201
26. DES.	POPHAND	9232	
	NIGRANA	3620	
	BAZCHIM	5637	18,489
27. ZAA.	SAZIAMI	7220	
	MATHVLA	7560	
	ORPAMB	7263	22,043
28. BAG.	LABNIXP	2360	
	FOCISNI	7236	
	OXLOPAR	8200	18,066
29. RII.	VASTRIM	9632	
	ODRAXTI	4236	
	GOMZIAM	7635	21,503
30. TEX.	TAONGLA	4632	
	GEMNIMB	9636	
	ADVORPT	7632	
	DOZINAL	5632	27,532

Plate X. shows us the names of these governors in the four Watch-Towers. Compare with Plate III.

Note that the sigil of each Governor is unique; the four sigils at the corners of Plate X. without the great square are those of the four great Elemental Kings:

Air **TAHAOELOJ**
Water **THAHEBYOBEEATAN**
Earth **THAHAAOTAHE**
Fire **OHOOOHAATAN**

The HOLY TABLE.

PLATE I.

71

SIGILLVM DEI ÆMETH.

PLATE II.

THE FOUR GREAT WATCH-TOWERS AND THE BLACK CROSS
WITHIN GENERAL VIEW.

PLATE III.

73

THE GREAT WATCH-TOWER OF THE EAST, ATTRIBUTED TO AIR.

PLATE IV.

74

THE GREAT WATCH-TOWER OF THE WEST, ATTRIBUTED TO WATER.

PLATE V.

THE GREAT WATCH-TOWER OF THE NORTH, ATTRIBUTED TO EARTH.

PLATE VI.

76

THE GREAT WATCH-TOWER OF THE SOUTH, ATTRIBUTED TO FIRE.

PLATE VII.

THE BLACK CROSS, OR TABLE OF UNION,
ATTRIBUTED TO SPIRIT.

PLATE VIII.

PLATE IX.

79

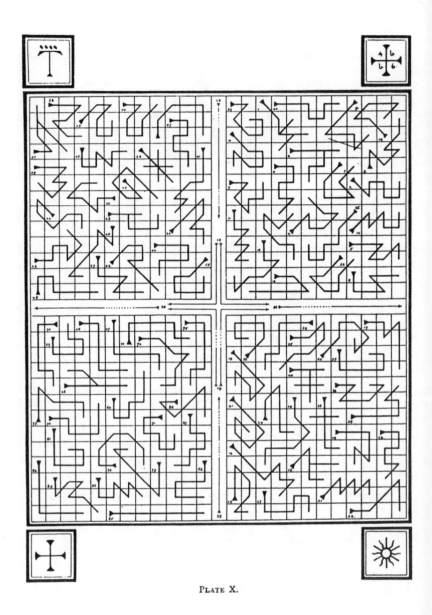

PLATE X.

PART II

THE FORTY-EIGHT CALLS OR KEYS

These are Most Solemn Invocations. Use these only after other invocations. Key tablet hath 6 calls, 1 above other 5.

1: Governs generally as a whole the tablet of Union. Use it *first* in all invocations of Angels of that tablet, but not at all with other 4 tablets.

2: Used as an invocation of Angels e h n b representing governance of Spirit in the tablet of Union: also precedes, *in the second place*, all invocations of Key tablet Angels. Not used in invocations of 4 other tablets.

3, 4, 5, 6: Used in invocations of Angels of Tablet of Union, *also* of angels of 4 terrestrial tablets, thus—

3: Used to invoke Angels of the letters of the line e x a r p.

For those of Tablet ORO as a whole and for the lesser angle of this tablet, which is that of the element itself, viz. i d o i g o. So for others—

The remaining 12 Keys refer to the remaining lesser angles of the tablets, the order of the elements being Air, Water, Earth, Fire.

Pronounce Elemental language (also called Angelic or Enochian) by inserting the next following Hebrew vowel between consonants, *e.g.* e after b (bEth), i after g (gImel), a after d, etc.

THE OPENING OF THE PORTAL
OF THE VAULT OF THE ADEPTS

PAROKETH, the Veil of the Sanctuary.
The Sign of the Rending of the Veil.
The Sign of the Closing of the Veil.
[Give these.]
Make the Invoking Pentagrams of Spirit.

In the number 21, in the grand word AHIH ;
In the Name YHShVH, in the Pass Word I.N.R.I.,

O Spirits of the Tablet of Spirit,
Ye, ye, I invoke!
The sign of Osiris slain!
The sign of the mourning of Isis!
The sign of Apophis and Typhon!
The sign of Osiris Risen!
L.V.X., Lux. The Light of the Cross.
[Give these.]

In the name of IHVH ALVH VDOTh, I declare that the
Spirits of Spirit have been duly invoked.
The Knock 1—4444.

THE FIRST KEY[1]

OL sonuf vaoresaji, gohu IAD Balata, elanusaha
caelazod: sobrazod-ol Roray i ta nazodapesad, Giraa ta
maelpereji, das hoel-qo qaa notahoa zodimezod, od
comemahe ta nobeloha zodien; soba tahil ginonupe
pereje aladi, das vaurebes obolehe giresam. Casarem
ohorela caba Pire: das zodonurenusagi cab: erem
Iadanahe. Pilahe farezodem zodenurezoda adana gono
Iadapiel das home-tohe: soba ipame lu ipamis: das
sobolo vepe zodomeda poamal, od bogira aai ta piape
Piamoel od Vaoan[2] ! Zodacare, eca, od zodameranu!
odo cicale Qaa; zodoreje, lape zodiredo Noco Mada,
Hoathahe I A I D A!

86 words in this Enochian Call.
[Invokes the whole Tablet of Spirit.]

---

[1]Collation of the various MSS. of these calls has not done
away with Various Readings; and there is not enough of the
language extant to enable a settlement on general principles. —
Ed.

[2] Read here Vooan in invocations of Fallen Spirits.

THE FIRST KEY

I REIGN over ye, saith the God of Justice, in power exalted above the Firmament of Wrath, in whose hands the Sun is as a sword, and the Moon as a through thrusting Fire: who measureth your Garments in the midst of my Vestures, and trussed you together as the palms of my hands. Whose seats I garnished with the Fire of Gathering, and beautified your garments with admiration. To whom I made a law to govern the Holy Ones, and delivered ye a Rod, with the Ark of Knowledge. Moreover you lifted up your voices and sware obedience and faith to Him that liveth and triumpheth: whose beginning is not, nor end cannot be: which shineth as a flame in the midst of your palaces, and reigneth amongst you as the balance of righteousness and truth!

Move therefore, and shew yourselves! Open the mysteries of your creation! Be friendly unto me, for I am the Servant of the same your God: the true worshipper of the Highest!

169 words in the English Call.

THE SECOND KEY

ADAGITA vau-pa-ahe zodonugonu fa-a-ipe salada! Vi-i-vau el! Sobame ial-pereji i-zoda-zodazod pi-adapehe casarema aberameji ta ta-labo paracaleda qo-ta lores-el-qo turebesa ooge balatohe! Giui cahisa lusada oreri od micalapape cahisa bia ozodonugonu! lape noanu tarofe coresa tage o-quo maninu IA-I-DON. Torezodu! gohe-el, zodacare eca ca-no-quoda! zodameranu micalazodo od ozadazodame vaurelar; lape zodir IOIAD!

THE SECOND KEY

CAN the Wings of the Winds understand your voices of Wonder? O you! the second of the First! whom the burning flames have framed in the depth of my Jaws! Whom I have prepared as cups for a wedding, or as the flowers in their beauty for the chamber of Righteousness! Stronger are your feet than the barren stone: and mightier are your voices than the manifold winds! For you are become a building such as is not, save in the Mind of the All-Powerful.

Arise, saith the First: Move therefore unto his servants! Shew yourselves in power, and make me a strong Seer-of-things: for I am of Him that liveth for ever!

[Invokes: The File of Spirit in the Tablet of Spirit.
  E — the Root of the Powers of Air.
  H — the Root of the Powers of Water.
  N — the Root of the Powers of Earth.
  B — the Root of the Powers of Fire.
    The Four Aces.]

THE OPENING OF THE TEMPLE IN THE GRADE OF 2° = 9°.

GIVE the Sign of Shu.

[Knock.] Let us adore the Lord and King of Air!
Shaddai El Chai! Almighty and ever-living One, be Thy Name ever magnified in the Life of All. (Sign of Shu.) Amen!

[Make the Invoking Pentagram of Spirit Active in these names: AHIH AGLA EXARP.]

[Make the Invoking Pentagram of Air in these names: IHVH ShDI AL ChI.]

And Elohim said: Let us make Adam in Our own image, after our likeness, and let them have dominion over the fowls of the air.

In the Names of IHVH and of ShDI AL ChI, Spirits of Air, Adore your Creator!

[With air-dagger (or other suitable weapon) make the sign of Aquarius.] In the name of RPAL and in the Sign of the Man, Spirits of Air, adore your Creator!

[Make the Cross.] In the Names and Letters of the Great Eastern Quadrangle, Spirits of Air, Adore your Creator!

[Hold dagger aloft.] In the Three great Secret Names of God, ORO IBAH AOZPI that are borne upon the Banners of the East, Spirits of Air, adore your Creator!

[Again elevate dagger.] In the Name of BATAIVAH, great King of the East, Spirits of Air, adore your Creator!

In the Name of Shaddai AL Chai, I declare that the Spirits of Air have been duly invoked.

The Knock 333—333—333.

THE THIRD KEY

MICAMA! goho Pe-IAD! zodir com-selahe azodien biabe os-lon-dohe. Norezodacahisa otahila Gigipahe; vaunud-el-cahisa ta-pu-ime qo-mos-pelehe telocahe; qui-i-inu toltoregi cahisa i cahisaji em ozodien; dasata beregida od torezodul! Ili e-Ol balazodareji, od aala tahilanu-os netaabe: daluga vaomesareji elonusa cape-mi-ali vaoresa *cala* homila; cocasabe fafenu izodizodope, od miinoagi de ginetaabe: vaunu na-na-e-el: panupire malapireji caosaji. Pilada noanu vaunalahe balata od-vaoan. Do-o-i-ape mada: goholore, gohus, amiranu! Micama! Yehusozod ca-ca-com, od do-o-a-inu noari micaolazoda a-ai-om. Casarameji gohia: Zodacare! Vaunigilaji! od im-ua-mar pugo pelapeli Ananael Qo-a-an.

Eighty words in the Enochian Call.

THE THIRD KEY

BEHOLD! saith your God! I am a circle on whose hands stand Twelve Kingdoms. Six are the seats of living breath: the rest are as sharp Sickles, or the Horns of Death. Wherein the creatures of Earth are and are not, except (in) mine own hands; which sleep and shall rise!

In the First I made ye stewards, and placed ye in twelve seats of government: giving unto every one of you power successively over the 456 true ages of time: to the intent that from the highest vessels and the corners of your governments you might work my Power, pouring down the fires of life and increase continually on the earth. Thus you are become the skirts of Justice and Truth.

In the name of the same your God, lift up, I say, yourselves!

Behold! His mercies flourish, and (His) Name is become mighty among us. In whom we say: Move! Descend! and apply yourselves unto us as unto the partakers of His Secret Wisdom in your Creation.

167 words in this English Call.

[Invokes: Exarp; the whole Tablet of Air.
   The angle of Air of Air.
   The Prince of the Chariot of the Winds.]

THE OPENING OF THE TEMPLE
IN THE GRADE OF 3° = 8□.

GIVE the Sign of Auramoth.

[Knock.] Let us adore the Lord and King of Water! Elohim Tzabaoth! Elohim of Hosts!

Glory be to the Ruach Elohim which moved upon the Face of the Waters of Creation!

AMEN!

[Make the Invoking Pentagram of Spirit Passive and pronounce these names: AHIH AGLA HCOMA.]

[Make the Invoking Pentagram of Water and pronounce: AL ALHIM TzBAVTh.]

And Elohim said: Let us make Adam in Our image; and let them have dominion over the Fish of the

Sea! In the Name of AL, Strong and Powerful, and in the name of ALHIM TzBAVTh, Spirits of Water, adore you Creator!

[Make Sigil of Eagle with cup.] In the name of GBRIAL and in the sign of the Eagle, Spirits of Water, adore your Creator!

[Make cross with cup.] In all the Names and Letters of the Great Quadrangle of the West, Spirits of Water, adore your Creator!

[Elevate cup.] In the three great Secret Names of God MPH ARSL GAIOL that are borne upon the Banners of the West, Spirits of Water, adore your Creator!

[Elevate cup.] In the Name of RAAGIOSEL, great King of the West, Spirits of Water, adore your Creator!

In the name of Elohim Tzabaoth, I declare that the Spirits of Water have been duly invoked.

The Knock. 1—333—1—333.

THE FOURTH KEY

OTAHIL elasadi babaje, od dorepaha gohol: gicahisaje auauago coremepe *peda*, dasonuf vi-vau-divau? Casaremi oeli *meapeme* sobame agi coremepo carep-el: casaremeji caro-o-dazodi cahisa od vaugeji; dasata ca-pi-mali cahisa ca-pi-ma-on: od elonusahinu cahisa ta el-o *calaa*. Torezodu nor-quasahi od fecaosaga: Bagile zodir e-na-IAD: das iod apila! Do-o-a-ipe quo-A-AL, zodacare! Zodameranu obelisonugi resat-el aaf nor-mo-lapi!

THE FOURTH KEY

I HAVE set my feet in the South, and have looked about me, saying: are not the thunders of increase numbered 33, which reign in the second Angle?

Under whom I have placed 9639: whom none hath yet numbered, but One; in whom the Second Beginnings of Things are and wax strong, which also successively are the Numbers of Time: and their powers are as the first 456.

Arise! you sons of Pleasure! and visit the earth: for I am the Lord your God; which is and liveth (for ever)! In the name of the Creator, move! and shew yourselves as pleasant deliverers, that you may praise him among the sons of men!

[Invokes: Hcoma; the whole tablet of Water.

The Angle of Water of Water.

The Queen of the Thrones of Water.]

THE OPENING OF THE TEMPLE IN THE GRADE OF 1° = 10º.

GIVE the Sign of the God SET fighting.

Purify with Fire and Water, and announce "The Temple is cleansed."

[Knock.] Let us adore the Lord and King of Earth!

Adonai ha Aretz, Adonai Melekh, unto Thee be the Kingdom, the Sceptre, and the Splendour: Malkuth, Geburah, Gedulah, The Rose of Sharon and the Lily of the Valley, Amen!

[Sprinkle Salt before Earth tablet.] Let the Earth adore Adonai!

[Make the Invoking Hexagram of Saturn.]

[Make the Invoking Pentagram of Spirit Passive, and pronounce these Names: AHIH AGLA NANTA.]

[Make the Invoking Pentagram of Earth, and pronounce this Name: ADNI MLK.]

And Elohim said: Let us make Man in Our own image; and let them have dominion over the Fish of the Sea and over the Fowl of the Air: and over every creeping thing that creepeth upon the Earth. And the Elohim created ATh-h-ADAM: in the image of the Elohim created They them; male and female created They them. In the Name of ADNI MLK, and of the

88

Bride and Queen of the Kingdom; Spirits of Earth, adore your Creator!

[Make the Sign of Taurus.] In the Name of AVRIAL, great archangel of Earth, Spirits of Earth, adore your Creator!

[Make the Cross.] In the Names and Letters of the Great Northern Quadrangle, Spirits of Earth, adore your Creator!

[Sprinkle water before Earth Tablet.] In the three great secret Names of God, MOR, DIAL, HCTGA, that are borne upon the Banners of the North, Spirits of Earth, adore your Creator!

[Cense the Tablet.] In the name of IC-ZOD-HEH-CA(L), great King of the North, Spirits of Earth, adore your Creator!

In the Name of Adonai Ha-Aretz, I declare that the Spirits of Earth have been duly invoked.

The Knock. 4444—333—22—1.

THE FIFTH KEY

SAPAHE zodimii du-i-be, od noasa ta qu-a-nis, adarocahe dorepehal caosagi od faonutas peripesol ta-be-liore. Casareme A-me-ipezodi na-zodaretahe *afa;* od dalugare zodizodope zode-lida caosaji tol-toregi; od zod-cahisa esiasacahe El ta-vi-vau; od iao-d tahilada das hubare *pe-o-al;* soba coremefa cahisa ta Ela Vaulasa od Quo-Co-Casabe. Eca niisa od darebesa quo-a-asa: fetahe-ar-ezodi od beliora: ia-ial eda-nasa cicalesa; bagile Ge-iad I-el!

THE FIFTH KEY

THE mighty sounds have entered into the third angle, and are become as olives in the Olive Mount; looking with gladness upon the earth, and dwelling in the brightness of the Heavens as continual Comforters.

Unto whom I fastened 19 Pillars of Gladness, and gave them vessels to water the earth with her creatures; and they are the brothers of the First and Second, and the beginning of their own seats, which are garnished with 69,636 ever-burning lamps: whose numbers are as the First, the Ends, and the Contents of Time.

Therefore come ye and obey your creation: visit us in peace and comfort: conclude us receivers of your mysteries: for why? Our Lord and Master is the All-One!

[Invokes: Nanta; the whole tablet of Earth.
The angle of Earth of Earth.
The Princess of the Echoing Hills,
The Rose of the Palace of Earth.]

THE OPENING OF THE TEMPLE IN THE GRADE OF 4° = 7□.

GIVE the sign of Thoum-aesh-neith.

[Knock.] Let us adore the Lord and King of Fire!
Tetragrammaton Tzabaoth! Blessed be Thou! The Leader of Armies is Thy Name! AMEN!

[Make the Invoking Pentagram of Spirit Active, and pronounce these Names: AHIH AGLA BITOM.]

[Make the Invoking Pentagram of Fire, and pronounce: ALHIM IHVH TzBAVTh.]

[Make the sign of Leo with censer (or other suitable weapon).] In the name of MIKAL, archangel of Fire, Spirits of Fire, adore your Creator!

[Make the Cross.] In the Names and Letters of the Great Southern Quadrangle, Spirits of Fire, adore your Creator!

[Elevate censer.] In the three Secret names of God, OIP TEAA PDOCE, that are borne upon the banners of the South, Spirits of Fire, adore your Creator!

[Lower and lift censer.] In the Name of EDELPERNA, great King of the South, Spirits of Fire, adore your Creator!

In the Name of IHVH TzBAVTh, I declare that the Spirits of Fire have been duly invoked.
The Knock. 333—1—333.

THE SIXTH KEY

GAHE sa-div cahisa *em*, micalazoda Pil-zodinu, sobam El haraji mir babalonu od obeloce samevelaji, dalagare malapereji ar-caosaji od *acame* canale, sobola zodare fa-beliareda caosaji od cahisa aneta-na miame ta Viv od Da. Daresare Sol-petahe-bienu. Be-ri-ta od zodacame ji-mi-calazodo: sob-ha-atahe tarianu luia-he od ecarinu MADA Qu-a-a-on!

THE SIXTH KEY

THE Spirits of the fourth angle are Nine, Mighty in the Firmament of Waters: whom the First hath planted, a torment to the wicked and a garland to the righteous: giving unto them fiery darts to vanne the earth, and 7699 continual workmen, whose courses visit with comfort the earth; and are in government and continuance as the Second and the Third—

Therefore hearken unto my voice! I have talked of you, and I move you in power and presence, whose works shall be a song of honour, and the praise of your God in your Creation!

[Invokes: Bitom; the whole tablet of Fire.
The Angle of Fire of Fire
The Lord of the Flame and the Lightning,
The King of the Spirits of Fire.]

THE SEVENTH KEY

RA-ASA isalamanu para-di-zoda oe-cari-mi aao iala-pire-gahe Qui-inu. Enai butamonu od inoasa *ni* pa-ra-diala. Casaremeji ujeare cahirelanu, od zodonace lucifatianu, caresa ta vavale-zodirenu tol-hami. Soba lonudohe od nuame cahisa ta Da o Desa vo-ma-dea od pi-beliare itahila rita od miame ca-ni-quola rita! Zodacare! Zodameranu! Iecarimi Quo-a-dahe od I-

mica-ol-zododa aaiome. Bajirele papenore idalu-gama
elonusahi—od umapelifa vau-ge-ji Bijil —IAD!

THE SEVENTH KEY

THE East is a house of Virgins singing praises
among the flames of first glory wherein the Lord hath
opened his mouth; and they are become 28 living
dwellings in whom the strength of man rejoiceth; and
they are apparelled with ornaments of brightness, such
as work wonders on all creatures. Whose kingdoms
and continuance are as the Third and Fourth, strong
towers and places of comfort, the Seats of Mercy and
Continuance. O ye Servants of Mercy, Move! Appear!
Sing praises unto the Creator; and be mighty amongst
us. For that to this remembrance is given power, and
our strength waxeth strong in our Comforter!

The Angle of Water of Air, in the tablet of Air.
The Queen of the Thrones of Air.

THE EIGHT KEY

BAZODEMELO i ta pi-ripesonu olanu Na-
zodavabebe *ox*. Casaremeji varanu cahisa vaugeji asa
berameji balatoha: goho IAD. Soba miame tarianu ta
lolacis Abaivoninu od azodiajiere riore. Irejila cahisa
da das pa-aox busada Caosago, das cahisa od ipuranu
telocahe cacureji o-isalamahe lonucaho od Vovina
carebafe? NIISO! bagile avavago gohon. NIISO!
bagile momao siaionu, od mabezoda IAD oi asa-
momare poilape. NIIASA! Zodameranu ciaosi caosago
od belioresa od coresi ta a beramiji.

THE EIGHTH KEY

THE Midday, the first is as the third Heaven made
of 26 Hyacinthine Pillars, in whom the Elders are
become strong, which I have prepared for mine own
Righteousness, saith the Lord: whose long
continuance shall be as bucklers to the Stooping
Dragon, and like unto the harvest of a Widow. How

many are there which remain in the Glory of the Earth, which are, and shall not see Death until the House fall and the Dragon sink? Come away! for the Thunders (of increase) have spoken. Come away! for the Crowns of the Temple and the Robe of Him that is, was, and shall be, crowned, are divided! Come forth! Appear! to the terror of the Earth, and to our comfort, and to the comfort of such as are prepared.

The Angle of Earth of Air, in the tablet of Air.
The Princess of the Rushing Winds,
the Lotus of the Palace of Air.

THE NINTH KEY

MICAOLI beranusaji perejela napeta ialapore, das barinu efafaje *Pe* vaunupeho olani od obezoda, soba-ca upaahe cahisa tatanu od tarananu balie, alare busada so-bolunu od cahisa hoel-qo ca-no-quodi *cial*. Vaunesa aladonu mom caosago ta iasa olalore ginai limelala. Amema cahisa sobra madarida zod cahisa! Ooa moanu cahisa avini darilapi caosajinu: od butamoni pareme zodumebi canilu. Dazodisa etahamezoda cahisa dao, od mireka ozodola cahisa pidiai Colalala. Ul ci ninu a sobame ucime. Bajile? IAD BALATOHE cahirelanu pare! NIISO! od upe ofafafe; bajile a-cocasahe icoresaka a uniji beliore.

THE NINTH KEY

A MIGHTY guard of Fire with two-edged swords flaming (which have eight Vials of wrath for two times and a half, whose wings are of wormwood and of the marrow of salt), have set their feet in the West, and are measured with their 9996 ministers. These gather up the moss of the Earth as the rich man doth his Treasure. Cursed are they whose iniquities they are! In their eyes are mill-stones greater than the earth, and from their mouths run seas of blood. Their heads are covered with diamonds, and upon their heads are marble stones[3] Happy is he on whom they frown not. For why? The Lord of Righteousness rejoiceth in them! Come away, and not your Vials: for that the time is such as requireth Comfort.

The Angle of Fire of Air, in the tablet of Air.
The Lord of the Winds and Breezes,
the King of the Spirits of Air.

THE TENTH KEY

CORAXO cahisa coremepe, od belanusa Lucala azodiazodore paebe Soba iisononu cahisa uirequo *ope* copehanu od racalire maasi bajile caosagi; das yalaponu dosiji od basajime; od ox ex dazodisa siatarisa od salaberoxa cynuxire faboanu. Vaunala cahisa conusata das *daox* cocasa ol Oanio yore vohima ol jizodyazoda od eoresa cocasaji pelosi molui das pajeipe, laraji same darolanu matorebe cocasaji emena. El pataralaxa yolaci matabe nomiji mononusa olora jinayo anujelareda. Ohyo! ohyo! ohyo! ohyo! ohyo! ohyo! noibe Ohyo! caosagonu! Bajile madarida i zodirope cahiso darisapa! NIISO! caripe ipe nidali!

THE TENTH KEY

THE Thunders of Judgement and Wrath are numbered and are harboured in the North, in the likeness of an Oak whose branches are 22 nests of lamentation and weeping laid up for the earth: which burn night and day, and vomit out the heads of scorpions and live Sulphur mingled with poison. These be the thunders that, 5678 times in the twenty-fourth part of a moment, roar with a hundred might earthquakes and a thousand times as many surges, which rest not, neither know any[4] time here. One rock bringeth forth a thousand, even as the heart of man doth his thoughts. Woe! Woe! Woe! Woe! Woe! Woe!

---

[3] v.l. "Upon their hands are marble sleeves."
[4] v.l. "Any echoing time between."

Yea, Woe be to the Earth, for her iniquity is, was, and shall be great. Come away! but not your mighty sounds!

The Angle of Air of Water, in the tablet of Water.
The Prince of the Chariot of the Waters.

THE ELEVENTH KEY

OXIAYALA holado, od zodirome *O* coraxo das zodiladare raasyo. Od vabezodire cameliaxa od bahala: NIISO! salamanu telocahe! Casaremanu hoel-qo, od ti ta zod cahisa soba coremefa i ga. NIISA! bagile aberameji nonuçape. Zodacare eca od Zodameranu! odo cicale Qaa! Zodoreje, lape zodiredo Noco Mada, hoathahe IAIDA!

THE ELEVENTH KEY

THE mighty Seat groaned, and there were five Thunders that flew into the East. And the Eagle spake and cried aloud: Come away from the House of Death! And they gathered themselves together and became (those) of whom it is measured, and it is as They are, whose number is 31. Come away! For I have prepared (a place) for you. Move therefore, and shew yourselves! Unveil the mysteries of your Creation. Be friendly unto me, for I am the servant of the same your God: the true worshipper of the the Highest.

The Angle of Earth of Water, in the tablet of Water.
The Princess of the Waters,
the Lotus of the Palace of the Floods.

THE TWELFTH KEY

NONUCI dasonuf Babaje od cahisa *ob* hubaio tibibipe: alalare ataraahe od ef! Darix fafenu *mianu* ar Enayo ovof! Soba dooainu aai i VONUPEHE. Zodacare, gohusa, od Zodameranu. Odo cicale Qaa! Zodoreje, lape zodiredo Noco Mada, hoathahe IAIDA!

95

THE TWELFTH KEY

O YE that range in the South and are the 28 Lanterns of Sorrow, bind up your girdles and visit us! bring down your train 3663 (servitors), that the Lord may be magnified, whose name amongst ye is Wrath. Move! I say, and shew yourselves! Unveil the mysteries of your Creation. Be friendly unto me, for I am the servant of the same your God, the true worshipper of the Highest.

The Angle of Fire of Water, in the tablet of Water.
The Lord of the Waves and the Waters,
the King of the Hosts of the Sea.

THE THIRTEENTH KEY

NAPEAI Babajehe das berinu *vax* ooaona larinuji vonupehe doalime: conisa olalogi oresaha das cahisa afefa. Micama isaro Mada od Lonu-sahi-toxa, das ivaumeda aai Jirosabe. Zodacare od Zodameranu. Odo cicale Qaa! Zodoreje, lape zodiredo Noco Mada, hoathahe IAIDA.

THE THIRTEENTH KEY

O YE Swords of the South, which have 42 eyes to stir up the wrath of Sin: making men drunken which are empty: Behold the Promise of God, and His Power, which is called amongst ye a bitter sting! Move and Appear! unveil the mysteries of your Creation, for I am the servant of the same your God, the true worshipper of the Highest.

The Angle of Air of Earth, in the tablet of Earth.
The Prince of the Chariot of Earth.

THE FOURTEENTH KEY

NORONI bajihie pasahasa Oiada! das tarinuta mireca *ol* tahila dodasa tolahame caosago *h*omida: das berinu orocahe *quare:* Micama! Bial' Oiad; aisaro toxa das ivame aai Balatima. Zodacare od Zodameranu!

Odo cicale Qaa! Zodoreje, lape zodiredo Noco Mada, hoathahe IAIDA.

THE FOURTEENTH KEY

O YE Sons of Fury, the Daughters of the Just One! that sit upon 24 seats, vexing all creatures of the Earth with age, that have 1636 under ye. Behold! The voice of God: the promise of Him who is called amongst ye Fury or Extreme Justice. Move and shew yourselves! Unveil the mysteries of your Creation; be friendly unto me, for I am the servant of the same your God: the true worshipper of the Highest!

The Angle of Water of Earth, in the tablet of Earth.
The Queen of the Thrones of Earth.

THE FIFTEENTH KEY

ILASA! tabaanu li-El pereta, casaremanu upaahi cahisa *dareji;* das oado caosaji oresacore: das omaxa monasaçi Baeouibe od emetajisa Iaiadix. Zodacare od Zodameranu! Odo cicale Qaa. Zodoreje, lape zodiredo Noco Mada, hoathahe IAIDA.

THE FIFTEENTH KEY

O THOU, the Governor of the first Flame, under whose wings are 6739; that weave the Earth with dryness: that knowest the Great Name "Righteousness," and the Seal of Honour. Move and Appear! Unveil the mysteries of your creation; be friendly unto me, for I am the servant of the same your God: the true worshipper of the Highest!

The Angle of Fire of Earth, in the tablet of Earth.
The Lord of the Wide and Fertile Land,
the King of the Spirits of Earth.

THE SIXTEENTH KEY

ILASA viviala pereta! Salamanu balata, das acaro odazodi busada, od belioraxa balita: das inusi caosaji lusadanu *emoda:* das ome od taliobe: darilapa iehe ilasa

Mada Zodilodarepe. Zodacare od Zodameranu. Odo cicale Qaa: zodoreje, lape zodiredo Noco Mada, hoathahe IAIDA.

THE SIXTEENTH KEY

O THOU second Flame, the House of Justice, which hast thy beginning in glory and shalt comfort the Just: which walkest upon the Earth with 8763 feet, which understand and separate creatures! Great art thou in the God of Stretch forth and Conquer. Move and appear! Unveil the mysteries of your Creation; be friendly unto me, for I am the servant of the same your God, the true worshipper of the Highest.

The Angle of Air of Fire, in the tablet of Fire.
The Prince of the Chariot of Fire.

THE SEVENTEENTH KEY

ILASA dial pereta! soba vaupaahe cahisa nanuba zodixalayo dodasihe od berinuta *faxisa* hubaro tasataxa yolasa: soba Iad *i* Vonupehe o Uonupehe: aladonu dax ila od toatare! Zodacare od Zodameranu! Odo cicale Qaa! Zodoreje, lape zodiredo Noco Mada, hoathahe IAIDA.

THE SEVENTEENTH KEY

O THOU third Flame! whose wings are thorns to stir up vexation, and who hast 7336 living lamps going before Thee: whose God is "Wrath in Anger": Gird up thy loins and hearken! Move and Appear! Unveil the mysteries of your Creation; be friendly unto me, for I am the servant of the same your God, the true worshipper of the Highest.

The Angle of Water of Fire, in the tablet of Fire.
The Queen of the Thrones of Flame.

THE EIGHTEENTH KEY

ILASA micalazoda olapireta ialpereji beliore: das odo Busadire Oiad ouoaresa caosago: casaremeji

Laiada *eranu* berinutasa cafafame das ivemeda aqoso
adoho Moz, od maof-fasa. Bolape como belioreta
pamebeta. Zodacare od Zodameranu! Odo cicale Qaa.
Zodoreje, lape zodiredo Noco Mada, hoathahe IAIDA.

THE EIGHTEENTH KEY

O THOU mighty Light and burning Flame of
Comfort! that unveilest the Glory of God to the centre
of the Earth, in whom the 6332 secrets of Truth have
their abiding, that is called in thy kingdom "Joy" and
not to be measured. Be thou a window of comfort unto
me! Move and Appear! Unveil the mysteries of your
Creation, be friendly unto me, for I am the servant of
the same your God, the true worshipper of the
Highest.

The Angle of Earth of Fire, in the tablet of Fire.
The Princess of the Shining Flame,
the Rose of the Palace of Fire.

MARK WELL!

THESE first 18 calls are in reality 19; that is, 19 in
the Celestial Orders; but with us the first table hath no
call, and can have no call, seeing that it is of the
Godhead. Thus, then, with us hath it the number of 0,
though with them that of 1. (Even as the first key of
the ROTA hath the number 0.)

After this follow the calls or keys of the Thirty
Aires or Æthyrs: which are in substance similar,
though, in the name of the Æthyrs, diversified.

The titles of the Thirty Æthyrs whose dominion
extendeth in ever-widening circles without and beyond
the Watch Towers of the Universe.

(The first is Outermost)

1	LIL	16	LEA
2	ARN	17	TAN
3	ZOM	18	ZEN

4	PAZ	19	POP
5	LIT	20	KHR
6	MAZ	21	ASP
7	DEO	22	LIN
8	ZID	23	TOR
9	ZIP	24	NIA
10	ZAX	25	VTI
11	ICH	26	DES
12	LOE	27	ZAA
13	ZIM	28	BAG
14	UTA	29	RII
15	OXO	30	TEX

THE CALL OR KEY OF THE THIRTY ÆTHYRS

MADARIATZA das perifa LIL[5]cahisa micaolazoda saanire caosago od fifisa balzodizodarasa Iaida. Nonuça gohulime: Micama adoianu MADA faoda beliorebe, soba ooaona cahisa luciftias peripesol, das aberaasasa nonuçafe netaaibe caosaji od tilabe adapehaheta damepelozoda, tooata nonuçafe jimicalazodoma larasada tofejilo marebe yareryo IDOIGO[6] od torezodulape yaodafe gohola, Caosaga, tabaoreda saanire, od caharisateosa yorepoila tiobela busadire, tilabe noalanu paida oresaba, od dodaremeni zodayolana. Elazodape tilaba pare-meji peripesatza, od ta qurelesata booapisa. Lanibame oucaho sayomepe, od caharisateosa ajitoltorenu, mireca qo tiobela lela. Tonu paomebeda dizodalamo asa pianu, od caharisateosa aji-la-tore-torenu paracahe a sayomepe. Coredazodizoda dodapala od fifalazoda, lasa manada, od faregita bamesa omaoasa. Conisabera od auauotza tonuji oresa; catabela noasami tabejesa leuitahemonuji. Vanucahi ome-petilabe oresa! Bagile? Moooabe OL coredazodizoda. El capimao itzomatzipe, od

---

[5] Or other Aire as may be willed.

[6] This name maybe appropriately varied with the Aire.

cacocasabe gosaa. Bajilenu pii tianuta a babalanuda, od faoregita teloca uo uime.

Madariiatza, torezodu!!! Oadariatza orocaha aboaperi! Tabaori periazoda aretabasa! Adarepanu coresata dobitza! Yolacame periazodi arecoazodiore, od quasabe qotinuji! Ripire paaotzata sagacore! Umela od peredazodare cacareji Aoiveae coremepeta! Torezodu! Zodacare od Zodameranu, asapeta sibesi butamona das surezodasa Tia balatanu. Odo cicale Qaa, od Ozodazodama pelapeli IADANAMADA!

THE CALL OR KEY OF THE THIRTY ÆTHYRS

O YE Heavens which dwell in the First Aire, ye are mighty in the parts of the Earth, and execute the Judgment of the Highest! Unto you it is said: Behold the Face of your God, the beginning of Comfort, whose eyes are the brightness of the Heavens, which provided you for the Government of the Earth, and her unspeakable variety, furnishing you with a power of understanding to dispose all things according to the Providence of Him that sitteth on the Holy Throne, and rose up in the Beginning, saying: The Earth, let her be governed by her parts, and let there be Division in her, that the glory of her may be always drunken, and vexed in itself. Her course, let it run with the Heavens; and as an handmaid let her serve them. One season, let it confound another, and let there be no creature upon or within her the same. All her members, let them differ in their qualities, and let there be no one Creature equal with another. The reasonable Creatures of the Earth, and Men, let them vex and weed out one another; and their dwelling-places, let them forget their Names. The work of man and his pomp, let them be defaced. His buildings, let them become Caves for the beasts of the Field! Confound her understanding with darkness! For why? it repenteth me that I have made Man. One while let her be known, and another while a stranger: because she is the bed of an Harlot, and the dwelling-place of him that is fallen.

O ye Heavens, arise! The lower heavens beneath you, let them serve you! Govern those that govern! Cast down such as fall. Bring forth with those that increase, and destroy the rotten. No place let it remain in one number. Add and diminish until the stars be numbered. Arise! Move! and appear before the Covenant of His mouth, which He hath sworn unto us in His Justice. Open the Mysteries of your Creation, and make us partakers of THE UNDEFILED KNOWLEDGE.

Finished are the Calls or Keys.

The Three Mighty Names of God
Almighty coming forth from
The Thirty Æthyrs

THE First Name—
LAZodaPeLaMeDaZodaZODaZodILaZodUOLaTa ZodaPe-KALaTaNuVaDaZodaBeReTa.

The Second Name—
IROAIAEIIAKOITaXEAEOHeSIOIITEAAIE.

The Third Name—
LaNuNuZodaTaZodODaPeXaHEMAOANuNuPe RePeNu-RAISAGIXa.

Ended are the Forty-eight Calls or Keys.

Chapter Six

Divine Eroticism

Intimate union of the worshipper with the Divine Principal is a central theme of religion. It is quite natural that the images which are evoked by the Devotee in his ardor for the Beloved are identical or similar to those that accompany sexual longings. The traditional cultures of India and the Orient, of Africa, Polynesia, of the natives of North and South America, indeed of almost any culture unpolluted by Judeo-Christian-Islamic thought, have no difficulty whatsoever with this parallel.

With the exception of the *Song of Solomon*, Western religious literature avoids Divine Eroticism like the plague. Even the esoteric disciplines of the West seem uncomfortable with the subject and go to great lengths to veil their terms. The bizarre nomenclature of Alchemy, when studied with half your brain in the bedroom, reveals that perhaps there are several good reasons why the alchemists were called "puffers". But for the most part, we in the West are expected to unite with our Divine Beloved vicariously.

Nuns are the "Brides of Christ", we unite with the Father or the Mother only "through the Son." Even the "magic" ceremony needed to consummate these voyeuristic unions must be experienced vicariously through a priest. In the highly explicit book *Taboo: "The Ecstacy of Evil" (The Psychopathology of Sex and Religion)* (New Falcon Publications, 1991), we explore the *abnormalities* of such practices and the psycho-sociological phobic reactions to Sex Magic.

I do not intend to use this space to serve as an introduction to the theories or techniques of Sex

103

Magick or Tantra. There are many fine works available
that introduce those subjects very well. For the reader
who is already knowledgeable on these subjects, a few
helpful hints concerning how Enochian can be used in
these areas may prove valuable and rewarding.

The modern view that our normal waking
consciousness stands somewhere between the limitless
potential of transcendental experience and the
"demons" that run amok in our subconscious mind is
not too dissimilar to the medieval view that Mankind is
sandwiched between God and the Angels, between
Heaven and Hell. The working hypothesis of the
magician of old went something like this, "God has
dominion over me and compels me to do His will. I
have dominion over the spirit world, (especially over
the so-called fallen angels), and just as I look up to
God, they look up to me, therefore I can compel them
to do my bidding."

In 1458, the noted Qabalist and court magician,
Abraham the Jew, in his classic work, *The Book of
the Sacred Magick of Abra-Melin The Mage*, took this
concept of the hierarchy of responsibility a sublime
step forward and catapulted magick to the same level
as the Yogic disciplines.

Simply put, to work the magick, you must first be
united with Divinity. (This experience he calls The
Knowledge and Conversation of the Holy Guardian
Angel.) This initiatory landmark is only accomplished
after a six month period of purification and a strict
regimen of ever-increasing longing for union with the
Angel. Once this "marriage" is consummated and the
"blessing" of the Angel's presence is bestowed, the
magician immediately turns to the lower spiritual world
and bestows the same "blessing" on the resident
denizens and extracts from them a pledge of loyalty
and support.

These wild and infernal spirits who, up until now were unacknowledged, uncontrolled and most likely at odds with the True Will of the magician, were now going to be given the opportunity to work for his and their greater good. And now that the magician had formed an intimate alliance with the Divine, he had the spiritual "authority" to force the lower spirits to cooperate.

Thus, Abraham the Jew reveals an indispensable truth; Magick demands an assault on two fronts at once. It requires realization of your responsibility not only to that which is above but also to that which is below.

It is only through *you* that the Divine (your Superconsciousness) can manifest on this plane. Without *you* the spirits of the Infernal regions (your subconsciousness) have no hope of "salvation" (balance and control). Indeed, without your controlling influence they will become a very real threat to your life and sanity. You must see to it that each area receives proper and equal attention. Neglect your higher aspiration and you will find that you soon lack the spiritual integrity to command the spirits. Neglect the spirits and they will sooner or latter surface to demand your attention. Wild beasts can be domesticated and trained to serve you. If you treat them well and allow them to share in your continuing good fortune they can realize their greater potentiality. However, if you abuse them or forget to feed them they will inevitably seize the first opportunity to break out and devour you for their needed nourishment.

The two pillars of the Enochian system, as outlined in *Liber Chanokh* are:

THE ELEMENTAL WATCH-TOWERS OF THE UNIVERSE AND THE TABLET OF UNION
THE WORLD OF THE ELEMENTAL BEINGS

THE THIRTY ÆTHYRS WHOSE DOMINION EXTENDETH IN EVER-
WIDENING CIRCLES WITHOUT AND BEYOND THE WATCH-
TOWERS OF THE UNIVERSE.

THE WORLD OF THE DIVINE BEINGS

Both these worlds can be explored sexually and can provide the diligent magician with the joy and fulfillment of his or her Divine Beloved and the passion and energy of being the Divine Beloved to an Elemental lover.

Please pay special attention to the following.

ENOCHIAN SEX MAGICK

But to love me is better than all things
Liber AL, I, 61

I will now proceed to ignore my own advice regarding other magician's visions. I hope the reader will recognize the value of what follows and will kindly forgive me.

In the series of visions of the 30 Æthyrs that Crowley chronicled in his remarkable work, *The Vision And The Voice*, he describes his vision of the Body of the great Goddess. The imagery is so powerful and his narrative colored with expressions of such tender awe, that one cannot but share, however temporarily, his overwhelming desire to unite with Her. To lose oneself utterly in Her would most certainly result in such intensity of bliss as to make the ecstasy of orgasm seem as a candle held up to the sun.

But that was Crowley's vision...Crowley's Great Goddess. To dwell on Her when you have your own Great Goddess (or God) "waiting" for your devotion would be as stupid as refusing a date with the lovely girl next door (who has secretly loved you all her life) because you have to sit at home alone, and pine over a painting of Helen of Troy.

Do you see where I'm heading with this? By a serious and concerted effort on your part, it is possible for you to achieve the highest level of spiritual experience your evolutionary-initiatory status will permit, including a relationship with the Divine Beloved. *Once you "know" Her (or Him) all subsequent "earthly" ecstasies take the form of devotional offerings to the Great Lover who rewards the devotee with increasingly sweeter embraces until finally the embrace is eternal.*

Where do you seek the initial Vision?

In yourself.

How can you start to look in yourself?

One way is by systematically skrying the 30 Æthyrs.

> *Nor let the fools mistake love; for there are love and love. There is the dove, and there is the serpent. Choose ye well!*
> *Liber AL, I,57*

In *The Little Mermaid*, Hans Christian Andersen writes of an Undine who is so enamored of a mortal man that she relinquishes her status as an immortal being for the opportunity to love and be loved by him. This charming tale contains a profound magical truth. Elemental spirits, whose natures are so specialized that they lack the balance of qualities necessary for sentient life, do indeed long for union with "complete" beings such as ourselves. Because their natures are universal they truly are immortal and if they should ever achieve union with a mortal they would actually "die" to their old, incomplete existence to be "born" into the life of their beloved. This is exactly what we do in our relationship with the Divine Principal.

The spirits of the Elemental Tablets are particularly suitable for such operations and all that is required is to call them up. It is so simple that you may set to work ill-prepared for success. A few words of caution might be in order.

Think before you proceed. Just what are you really prepared to handle? Experience has shown that it is most often wisest to contact a spirit from very low in the elemental hierarchy for operations such as this. Also, as in the everyday world, it is unwise to try to juggle too many of these relationships at the same time. If you think "Hell hath no fury like that of a *woman* scorned," think again. And sometimes jealousy *really is* a *green-eyed monster.*

Finally, and most importantly, *Never confuse your love for the Divine with your love for the Elemental.* The sexual "role" the magician assumes when making love to the Goddess (or God) is diametrically different than the "role" he or she plays when mating with an elemental spirit. In the former, the magician's attitude is that of adoration and awe and release is a gift from above, the result of ecstatic surrender. (To assume that attitude with an elemental lover would be spiritual suicide.) The sexual "role" the magician assumes with the elemental is one of loving dominance. The Spirit surrenders to you. You bestow your ecstasy as a gift and allow your elemental partner to share, through you, the Divine love.

Confusing these two "loves" is surely the fountainhead of all the ills sexual repression has visited upon mankind. If it is your Will to be a sex magician, see to it that you use your magick to face and conquer your life, not to hide from it.

Chapter Seven

Techniques Of Enochian Sex Magick

By Christopher S. Hyatt, Ph. D.

There is no evidence that the communicating Angels that delivered the Enochian system to Dr. John Dee and Edward Kelly ever instructed them concerning sexual applications of the art.

Biographers will be quick to point out the famous incident of April 1587 when, according to Kelly, the Angel Madimi suggested to Kelly that he and Dr. Dee share their wives in common. (Dee was absent during this communication). Enochian scholars argue that the text of this communication contains many flaws that do not characterize other less *personal* communications and that this may have been a case of magical wishful thinking on Kelly's part. Nevertheless it seems they did indeed swap wives and in spite of obvious attempts to erase the manuscript, the record confirms this. It seems the only "magical" result of this "operation" was the break up of Dee and Kelly as magical partners and the close of one of the most remarkable chapters in magical history.

To those knowledgeable in the theory and techniques of Tantra the keys of the Enochian system open a treasure-house of practical applications.

The exercises outlined below should be practiced only after you have a thorough mastery of the system in all its non-sexual applications. Any uncertainties on the part of the magician as to what he or she is doing will destroy needed concentration and create a "break" which will absorb the entire force of the operation. (In sexual workings that could be an overabundant amount

of energy particularly if you perform the exercises in
my Tantra book.)

EXPLORATION OF THE
THIRTY ÆTHYRS

*As written earlier in the text, the Thirty
Æthyrs are the "heavens" or Aires of the
system. Starting with the 30th Æthyr and
working to the 1st, the Magician explores only
as far as his or her personal level of Initiation
will permit. This process is comparable to
"pathworkings" of the Qabalistic system. In
Enochian terms, the "Great Work" of the
magician is to master all 30 Æthyrs. (Starting
with 30 and ending with 1) Experiences with
the 30 Æthyrs are highly personal and entirely
unique to each magician. Working with the
Æthyrs can be a lifetime endeavor and it is
entirely presumptuous and inappropriate for
another individual to "guide" another in this
area.*

This personal aspect of the Æthyrs coupled with
the simplicity of its "one-Call-does-it-all" procedure
makes it ideal for preliminary workings.

The great stumbling block to exploring the Æthyrs
is the difficulty one encounters in "breaking through"
to the next Æthyr. In the higher levels this may be
because the magician has reached his or her initiatory
limit. But in the lower Æthyrs it is more often the case
that the magician simply can't "let go" and refocus his
or her attention to the section of the brain where the
vision is taking place. In *Secrets of Western Tantra* I
provide an entire array of exercises which will help the
Magician "let go."

The following exercise is intended exclusively for
workings of the Thirty Æthyrs. There are two
participants whom we will refer to as the Magician and
the Assistant. For our illustration the male participant
is the Magician and will recite the Call and "receive"

110

the vision, the female participant is the Assistant and will eventually record the vision. These gender roles are for illustration only. The Magician can just as easily be female and the Assistant male. This particular operation is equally effective for participants of the same sex and can also be adapted for solitary workings. *It makes absolutely no difference who is Magician and who is Assistant.* It is only important that the couple decide before the operation commences.

Note: There must be no ambiguity about the willingness of either participant to take part in an operation of this kind. If one participant has to be coerced, begged or tricked into participation the vortex of ill-will that will emanate from the offended party will insure not only the failure of the operation but also the destruction of a more precious "magical asset", the respect of another human being.

EXAMPLE:

The Magician wishes to explore the 30th Æthyr, **TEX**, and the Assistant has expressed to him that it is her Will to participate in the operation.

Both participants bathe and dress at first in simple, soft, white garments. You may light incense, burn candles or use lights or soft music to enhance the mood. Small amounts of alcohol are also useful.

Prepare the room in which you are working with the appropriate symbols for the Æthyr such as the sigils of the Governors or the Elemental Tablet from which they are taken. In the case of **TEX** it would be the Water Tablet. (One couple I know has the Elemental Tablets and the Tablet of Union constructed entirely of wooden pyramids which they painstakingly have painted and lettered in Enochian. These are placed on the floor, under their bed, prior to æthyric or elemental workings.)

Begin by performing the Lesser Banishing Ritual of the Pentagram in the area in which you will be working. (The student is referred to the Appendix section of this book for additional instructions.)

THE LESSER BANISHING RITUAL
OF THE PENTAGRAM

The Qabalistic Cross

facing east:

Touch your forehead and say **Atoh (aah - toh)**

Touch your Heart and say **Malkuth (mal - kooth)**

Touch your Right Shoulder and say **Ve-Geburah (veh - ghee - boo - rah)**

Touch your Left Shoulder and say **Ve-Gedulah (veh - ghee - doo - lah)**

Touch your Heart and say **Le-Olam (lee - oh - lum)**

Point the symbolic dagger inward and say **Amen (aah - mayn)**.

Still facing east:

Trace the Banishing pentagram of Earth and vibrate **YHVH (yoad — hay — vaahv — hay)**, as you thrust your symbolic dagger into the heart of the pentagram.

With your arm still extended,
turn to the South:

Trace the Banishing pentagram of Earth and vibrate the name **ADONAI (aah — doh — noy)**. {Remember to thrust the symbolic dagger as you vibrate each God name}.

With your arm still extended,
turn to the West:

Trace the Banishing pentagram of Earth and vibrate the name **EHIEH** (eh — hayh — yay).

With your arm still extended,
turn to the North:

Trace the Banishing pentagram of Earth and vibrate the name **AGLA (ah — guh — lah).**

With your arm still extended return to the East, completing the circle. Now Imagine yourself surrounded in a Flaming Circle of four Pentagrams.

Stand straight with your arms out forming the shape of a Cross:

Say:

Before me **Raphael (rah - fay - ale)**
Behind me **Gabriel (gah - bree - ale)**
At my right shoulder, **Michael (mee-khigh - ale)**
At my left shoulder, **Auriel (oh - ree - ale)**

Then Say:

Before me **flames the Pentagram**
Behind me shines the **six-rayed Star**.

Finish by repeating the Qabalistic Cross:

Touch your forehead and say **Atoh**
Touch your Heart and say **Malkuth**
Touch your Right Shoulder and say **Ve-Geburah**
Touch your Left Shoulder and say **Ve-Gedulah**
Touch your Heart and say **Le-Olam**
Point the symbolic dagger inward and say **Amen.**

(See the Appendix for examples of the invoking and banishing Pentagrams of all the Elements which are used in Elemental Temple openings and invocations).

The Magician then recites the Call of the 30th Æthyr, **TEX**, (Madariatza das perifa **TEX**... etc.) while the Assistant simply relaxes and meditates upon the sounds of the Enochian Call.

When the Call is completed let the Magician slowly vibrate the names of the Governors. (In the case of **TEX** there are four Governors. All other Æthyrs have three.)

Then, (believe it or not), forget about the operation. Relax, take your time and enjoy each other's company. Build slowly and naturally to greater levels of arousal. Continue to do everything you can to sustain your love making (At least 25 minutes, but for God's sake don't keep looking at your watch!). The idea is to become joyfully and totally exhausted. Then at the moment of orgasm (and not a split second before) let the Magician remember the purpose of the operation (the Skrying of the Æther) and repeat the first line of the Call; **Madariatza das perifa TEX cahisa micaolazoda saanire caosago od fifsa balzodizodarasa Iaida.** This may be done verbally or mentally but it must be well memorized so that it can come forth effortlessly.

(Note: A tape recorder can be used for both repeating Calls and taking notes. Sometimes two recorders are very handy, one for taking notes and the other for playing Calls).

The Magician then falls exhausted and allows the flood of images to wash through his brain. The temptation to fall asleep will be almost irresistible and that is where the skill of the Assistant is most vital.

After a few quiet moments if the Magician is not relating his vision to the Assistant she must take it upon herself to question him. This requires a high degree of tact and subtlety for she does not want to disturb the vision and yet she cannot allow him to fall into a deeper state of unconsciousness. This takes practice. She should have a pad of paper and a pencil handy and should write down everything that the Magician says. She should be especially careful to correctly spell any unknown words or phrases and she should not hesitate to ask the Magician (or the entity speaking through the Magician) the correct spelling of Angelic words.

If the vision stalls and reaches a point where nothing further is happening the Assistant can sometimes give it a push.

EXAMPLE

Magician:All I see is a bunch of trees. Nothing is happening.

Assistant:Try turning around. Do you see anything now?

Magician:Just more trees but there is a small pond in the middle.

Assistant:Walk over to the pond. Look in the pond and tell me what you see.

Magician:At first I see only my own reflection but as I keep looking I see that the pond is actually a bowl supported by the wings of four Angels. etc.

If angels or other beings appear in the vision they must be tested by repeating the names of the Governors one at a time. If the entity shows discomfort at the name of any of the Governors dismiss it by continuing to repeat the Governor's name until it disappears and a being appears that is strengthened by hearing the names.

Do not be afraid of anything you "see" or "hear". Maintain an attitude of good natured tolerance even if hideous sights or terrifying beings or creatures appear.

Act like a dispassionate explorer. *Fear is failure and the forerunner of failure.*

When it is clear that the vision is finished, or when it is obvious that the Magician is now fatigued or ready to fall asleep it is time to end the operation.

It is of the utmost importance that the Magician now "snap out of it" for it is he who must banish and close the Temple. If the Magician is reluctant to "wake up" and perform his duties it is the Assistant's responsibility to *see that he does.* No effort should be spared to "break the spell" and return the Magician to the objective world. Turn on the lights, talk loudly, get a drink, or splash some water on your face.

Finally, he performs the Lesser Banishing Ritual of the Pentagram and the Magician and the Assistant review the notes and transfer them to the Magician's diary. The comments of the Assistant are often extremely important and should not be omitted in the record.

Often the couple will wish to change roles and explore the same Æthyr on a subsequent occasion. Allow at least one day between operations.

ELEMENTAL OPERATIONS
AND CREATION OF THE MAGICKAL CHILD

Dr. Israel Regardie believed that certain sex magick techniques could be used by advanced students to incarnate "spiritual" energies on the physical plane, as well as making important shifts in the orientation of the Psyche and the Universe. In other words, if these methods were used properly, couples could bring into the world "divine" forces in the children they generated, who could influence the future of the race.

In addition to creating "real children" these methods could be used to create "bio-psycho-spiritual vessels", which would shift the focus of the mind as well as develop new powers and abilities.

116

The creation of the magickal child by ritualized sexual practices is symbolic in one sense of the whirling forces of nature, mixing and separating in their chaotic dance of creation.

This mixing and separating process is vividly displayed in the Elemental Tablets and the Tablet of Union of the Enochian system. Working with these basic forces of nature allows conscious co-operation and co-creating with the cosmos, and the magician becomes a miniature form of the cosmic process following its root law.

By willful and conscious co-operation the magician increases and refines his energies, sacrificing himself or herself willingly to Nature instead of being a passive food source in the spiritual food chain. The realization that man's emotional, physical and sexual energies are food for the "gods" can create great personal turmoil at first, however when one begins to joyously participate in the spiritual feeding frenzy, one is "elevated perpendicularly to infinity."

SELECTING THE MAGICKAL CHILD
THE ENOCHIAN METHOD

The selection process is the most difficult and, in truth, the most magickal, aspect of the operation. The "soul searching" necessary for such an important act is awesome and should not be embarked upon with a frivolous attitude.

The Enochian adept (and no other should embark upon such project) is intimately familiar with every area of the Elemental environment and with his or her current initiatory position relative to the Thirty Æthyrs. By reviewing his or her personal diaries of perhaps hundreds of non sexual Enochian workings, the Magician can determine the areas of the system that manifest the qualities which are desirable in the magickal child.

117

For the purpose of our illustration we will say that we wish create a magickal child of purity and beauty. A child capable of reflecting and transmitting energy and impressions without being affected. A child such as this might be a great actor or politician because in this child others see themselves reflected. This is charming and disarming to others because when they look at the child they will see only what they want to see.

By checking the records of our previous evocations we see that **TDIM**, the Kerub ruling the *Water* Subangle of *Water* is the perfect Spirit to manifest in such a child.

The technique as outlined below has been adapted from the exercise The Orgastic Circulation of Light and is an excellent example of Tantric Enochian evocation.

In Dr. Regardie's copy of Wilhelm's *Secret Of The Golden Flower,* 3rd impression, 1935, there are a number of passages underlined. Dr. Regardie was not a habitual underliner, thus we may assume that when he did underline it was for a very good reason. One of the passages which he underlined more than once contained references to the circulation of light.

In the next method, the proper circulation of light is essential for true magickal effects to occur and has been modified for use in creating the magickal child. It is urged that the partners should practice the ritual many times *prior* to including the sexual aspects. As a rule it is wise to practice this together holding hands or touching in some fashion.

At the time determined most auspicious for the conception of the magickal child the Temple is made ready, Banished, Cleansed and Consecrated.

The Temple is then opened in the Grade of $3° = 8^{\square}$ as outlined in *Chanokh* and the two participants recite a brief Oath declaring their intention to perform this creative act.

PART I
THE GREAT WHIRLINGS

The male should be on his back and the female should sit on top of him. Move only when instructed, unless the penis begins to lose its stiffness.

Begin by imagining a *scintillating white light* about the size of a small basketball forming above the head and piercing the top of the skull. This is called the Kether point. Now vibrate the Three Holy Names of God (from the Water Tablet). **MPH ARSL GAIOL** as the sphere of Light grows brighter and more energetic. Do this for five minutes.

On the last six vibrations of **MPH ARSL GAIOL** the female should move on each sound of the Names.

As the force of this whirling ball of power becomes exceedingly real for you and your partner, allow the energy to descend slowly through the head. Allow it to rest in the throat or Da'ath point. Here imagine a *lavender color*. Vibrate the Name of the Great Elemental King of Water, **RAAGIOSL** until the energy becomes exceedingly real for you and your partner.

Again on the last six vibrations of **RAAGIOSL** the female should move six times.

Bring the energy down through the chest until it rests at the Heart or Tiphareth. Vibrate the Names of the six Seniors of the Water Tablet, **SAIINOV, SOAIZNT, LAOAZRP, LIGDISA, SLGAIOL, LSRAHPM**. The color of light should be *golden yellow* growing brighter and clearer as you vibrate each Name.

On the six last vibrations of the names of the Seniors the female should move six times.

Move the power through the diaphragm and abdominal region to the pelvis (Yesod), and vibrate the Divine Names of the Calvary Cross, Water of Water, **NELAPR**, **OMEBB** visualizing a sphere of *deep purple.*

Here on the last ten vibrations of **NELAPR** and **OMEBB** the male should move ten times very slowly.

Finally, allow the energy to descend through the legs until it formulates at Malkuth, the feet. Both participants vibrate the name of the Kerub, the Name of their magickal child **TDIM** visualizing a *black* sphere.

The male should again move ten times quickly on the final vibrations of the Child's name.

Now, draw the energy up from the Black light of Malkuth changing colors as described above as it ascends to Kether. When the light reaches Kether concentrate on the White brilliance of this region.

When the light is at Kether and your movements are complete, meditate silently for a few moments and then begin the circulation of white light.

Note: At times Dr. Regardie ignored the different colors of the Spheres and simply used the white scintillating light of Kether for each of the points. However, he and I agreed that the colored system is better suited for the practice of Sex Magick.

PART II
THE ORGASTIC CIRCULATION OF LIGHT

Circulate the energy of the the White Light as follows:

Allow it to descend downward and outward via the left side of the body during every exhalation. When it reaches the left foot, transfer the energy over to the right foot and allow it to ascend the right side of the body on the inhalation. This should be done at least 10 times. The partners should move slowly in unison 10 times.

The second circulation of energy begins in Kether and travels down the front of the body on the exhalation and then up the back of the body on the inhalation. This should be done at least ten times as well. The partners should move slowly in unison ten times.

The third circulation, beginning with Kether follows down through the body on the exhalation until it reaches Malkuth. The energy is drawn up through the body to Kether on the inhalation. When it reaches the Crown, imagine it to discharge like water from a fountain, at the end of each inhalation. The fire and sparks of this scintillating fountaining go up and out through the Crown and then descend down and encompasses the body on the exhalation. After the final circulation has been completed and the fountaining maintained for a few movements, the couple should begin moving and breathing heavily as they surround themselves with sparkling light. The movements should then become spontaneous and at the moment of orgasm the light should be gathered and thrust beyond Sahasrara, toward the Chakra with No Name.

PART III
THE CRYSTALLIZATION OF THE LIGHT

The orgastic Light of the Chakra of No Name may be likened to the Philosopher's Stone, The Golden Flower, or the Lotus. It is a body of light created by the process of transmutation of spiritual-sexual energy and is the womb of the magickal child. This is an experiential realization, thus, the proof of the pudding is in the Doing and Creating.

The process of transmutation requires the proper balance and mixing of heat and cold, passive and active, and white and black. In a broader sense we are using tremendous active forces to create a non-active force. The nurturing we provide the womb-child through our practices creates a worthy resting place of deep silence for the aspirants involved in the creation process.

The circulating of orgastic light is no doubt one of the most beautiful secrets of the Great Work. As the light circulates again and again and your practices become more powerful and refined, a crystallization occurs and you begin to form the magickal child. Whether you choose it to be physical or spiritual or both, the creation of this spirit body allows you to have contact with the forces of the higher Spiritual Body. You have not only opened the doors of perception, but can now begin the process of real action in a way unknown to those who lack this initiation.

Chapter Eight

The Enochian Dictionary

A

WORDS	PHONETIC	ENGLISH
Aaf	(Ah-ahff)	Amongst
Aai (AAo)	(Ah-ah-ee)	Amongst
Aaiom	(Ah-ah-ee-ohm)	Amongst us
Aala	(Ah-ah-lah)	Placed you
Abaivonin	(Ah-bah-ee-voh-nee-noo)	Stooping Dragon
Abila (Apila)	(Ah-bee-lah)	Liveth forever
Aboapri	(Ah-boh-ah-pay-ree)	Let them serve you
Abraassa	(Ah-brah-ah-ess-sah)	Provided
Abrang	(Ah-brah-noo-gee)	I have prepared
ACAM	(Ah-kahm)	7,6,9,9
Adgt	(Ah-dah-gee-tay)	Can
Adna	(Ah-dah-nah)	Obedience
Adohi	(Ah-doh-hee)	Kingdom
Adoian	(Ah-doh-ee-ah-noo)	Face
Adphaht	(Ah-dah-pay-hah-tay)	Unspeakable
Adroch	(Ah-dah-rohk-hay)	Olive Mount
Adrpan	(Ah-dah-ra-pahn-noo)	Cast down
Af	(Ah-eff)	Nineteen
Affa	(Ah-eff-fah)	Empty
Ag	(Ah-gee)	None, No
Aglo	(Ah-gloh)	In Thy
Alar	(Ah-lahr)	Have set
Aldi	(Ah-el-dee)	Of gathering
Aldon	(Ah-el-doh-noo)	Gather up, Gird
Allar	(Ah-el-lahr)	Bind up
Am	(Ah-em)	Beginning
Amipzi	(Ah-mee-pay-zoad-ee)	I fastened
Amiram	(Ah-mee-rahm)	Yourselves
Amis	(Ah-meess)	End
Amma	(Ah-em-mah)	Cursed
Ananael	(Ah-nah-nah-el)	Secret Wisdom
Anetab	(Ah-nay-tahb)	In government

Angelard	(Ah-nu-gee-lahr-dah)	His Thoughts
Aoiveae	(Ah-oh-ee-vay-ah-ay)	Stars
Ar	(Ah-ray)	To Vanne
Ar	(Ah-ray)	That (in order)
(Ar) Tabas	(Tah-bahs)	That Govern
ARN	(Ah-rah-noo)	2nd Aethyr
As	(Ah-ess)	Was
ASP	(Ah-ess-pay)	21st Aethyr
Aspt	(Ah-ess-pay-tay)	Before
Ath	(Ah-tay-hay)	Works
Atraah	(Ah-tay-rah-ah)	Your Girdles
Audcal	(Ah-vah-dah-kahl)	Mercury
Avavaco	(Ah-vah-vah-koh)	Thunders of increase
Avavox	(Ah-vah-vohx)	His pomp
Aviny	(Ah-vee-nee)	Millstones
Aziagier	(Ah-zoad-ee-ah-gee-ayr)	Harvest
Aziazor	(Ah-zoad-ee-ah-zoad-ohr)	Likeness
Azieh	(Ah-zoad-ee-ay)	Whose hands

B

Babage (n)	(Bah-bah-gay)	South
Babalon (d)	(Bah-bah-lohn)	Wicked (harlot)
Baeouib	(Bah-ay-oh-veeb)	Righteousness
BAG	(Bah-gee)	28th Aethyr
Baghie	(Bah-gee-hee-ay)	Fury
Bable (r)	(Bah-bay-lay)	For, Because, For Why?
Bahal	(Bah-hah-lah)	Cried loudly
Balit	(Bah-leet)	The Just
Balt (an)	(Bah-lay-tay)	Justice
Baltim	(Bah-lay-teem)	Extreme Justice
Baltoh	(Bah-lay-toh)	The Righteous
Baltoha	(Bah-lay-toh-hah)	For my own righteousness
Balye	(Bah-lee-ay)	Salt
Balzarg	(Bah-lay-zoad-ar-gee)	Stewards, Presidents
Bal-zizras	(Bah-lay Zoad-ee-zoad-rahs)	Judgement
Bams	(Bahm-ess)	Let them forget
Basgim	(Bahs-geem)	Day
Bazm (elo)	(Bah-zoad-em)	Mid-day
Bia (l)	(Bee-ah)	Voices
Biah	(Bee-ah)	Stand

Bien	(Bee-ay-nu)	My voice
Bigliad	(Beeg-lee-ah-dah)	In our comforter
Blans	(Blah-noo-ess)	Harboured
Blior	(Blee-ohr)	Continual comforters
Bliora	(Blee-oh-rah)	Comfort
Bliorax	(Blee-oh-rahx)	Shall comfort
Bliors	(Blee-oh-ray-ess)	Our comfort
Bogpa	(Boh-gee-pah)	Reigneth
Bolp	(Boh-lah-pay)	Be thou
Booapis	(Boh-oh-pees)	Let her serve them
Bramg	(Bay-ray-mee-gee)	Are prepared
Bransg	(Bay-ray-ness-gee)	Guard
Brgow	(Bay-rah-goh-vah)	Sleep
Brin	(Bay-reen)	Have
Brint	(Bay-reen-tay)	Hast
Busd	(Boos-dah)	Glory
Busdir	(Boos-dee-ray)	Glory
Butmon	(Boot-tay-mohn)	His mouth hath opened
Butmoni	(Boot-tay-moh-nee)	Their mouths

C

C	(Kah)	Unto, with
Cab	(Kah-bay)	Rod
Cacacom	(Kah-kah-cohm)	Flourish
Cacocasp	(Kah-koh-cahs-pay)	Another while
Cafafm	(Kah-fah-fahm)	Their abiding
Calz	(Kah-lah-zoad)	The firmament
Cam(piao)	(Kah-em)	While
Camliax	(Kah-em-lee-ahx)	Spake
Canal	(Kah-nah-lah)	Workmen
Caosg (o)	(Kah-oh-ess-gee)	The Earth
Capimaon	(Kah-pee-mah-oh-nu)	Numbers of Time
Capimi-ali	(Kah-pee-mee ah-lee)	Successively
Carbaf	(Kah-ray-bahf)	Sink
Cars (Cors)	(Kah-ress)	Such
Casarm	(Kah-sah-raym)	To Whom
Casarman	(Kah-sah-ray-mah-nu)	Under whose
Casarmg	(Kah-sah-ray-em-gee)	To Whom
Ceph	(Kay-pay-hay)	Title of (z)
Chirlan	(Kah-hee-ray-lah-nu)	Rejoiceth

Chis (or Chris)	(Kah-hees)	Are
Chisdao	(Koh-hees-dah-oh)	Diamonds
Chiso	(Kah-hee-soh)	Shall be
CHR	(Kay-hay-ray)	20th Aethyr
Cial	(Kee-ah-lah)	9, 9, 9, 6
Ciaosi	(Kee-ah-oh-see)	Terror
Cicle	(Kee-kah-lay)	Mysteries of Creation
Cla	(Kee-lah)	4, 5, 6.
Cnila	(Kee-nu-lah)	Blood
Caozior	(Koh-ah-zoad-ee-ohr)	Increase
Cocasb	(Koh-kah-see-bay)	Time
Colis	(Koh-lees)	Making
Collal	(Koh-lay-lahl)	Stones
Commah	(Kohm-mah)	Bindeth, trussed together
Como	(Koh-moh)/	A window
Comselh	(Kohm-say-lay-hay)	A circle
Conisbra	(Koh-nees-bay-rah)	The work of man
Const	(Kohn-ess-tay)	Thunders
Cophan	(Koh-pay-hah-nu)	Lamentation
Cor	(Koh-ray)	Number
Coraxo	(Koh-rah-x-oh)	Thunders of judgement
Cordiziz	(Koh-ray-dee-zoad-ee-zoad)	Reasonable creatures of earth, men
Cormp	(Koh-ray-em-pay)	Numbered
Cormp	(Koh-ray-em-pay)	Hath yet numbered
Cormpt	(Koh-ray-em-pay-tay)	Be numbered
Crcrg	(Kah-ray-kah-ray-gee)	Until
Cri-mi	(Kah-ree mee)	Praises
Cro-od-zi	(Koh-roh oh-dah zoad-ee)	The 2nd Beginning
C-rp (crip)	(Kah Ar-pay)	But

D

D (Dial)	(Dah)	Third
Da	(Dah)	There
Damploz	(Dah-me-pay-loh-zoad)	Variety
DAOX	(Dah-oh-x)	5, 6, 7, 8
Darbs	(Dah-ray-bah-ess)	Obey
DARG	(Dah-ray-gee)	6, 7, 3, 9
Darr	(Dar-ray-ray)	Philosopher's Stone
Darsar	(Dah-ray-sahr)	Wherefore

Dax	(Dahx)	Loins
Dazis	(Dah-zoad ees)	Their Heads
De	(Day)	Of
DEO	(Day-oh)	7th Aethyr
DES	(Day-ess)	26th Aethyr
Diu	(Dee-vah)	Angle
Dlafod	(Dah-lah-foh-dah)	Sulphur
Dluga (Dlagar)	(Dah-loo-gah)	Giving
Dlugam	(Dah-loo-gahm)	Given
Dlugar	(Dah-loo-gahr)	Gave them
Do	(Doh)	In
Doalim	(Doh-ah-leem)	Sin
Dobix	(Doh-beex)	Fall
Dodpal	(Doh-dah-pah-el)	Let them vex
Dods	(Doh-dahs)	Vexing
Dodseh	(Doh-dah-say-hay)	Vexation
Dooain (or p)	(Doh-oh-ah-ee-noo)	His name
Don	(Doh-noo)	Title of letter E (r)
Dorpha	(Doh-ray-pay-hah)	Have looked about me
Dorphal	(Doh-ray-pay-hahl)	Looking with gladness
Dosig	(Doh-see-gee)	Night
Drilpi (a)	(Dah-ree-lah-pah)	Great
Drix	(Dah-ree-x)	Bring down
Droln	(Dah-roh-lah-noo)	Any
Ds	(Dah-ess)	Who, that or which
Du-i-b (Duiv)	(Doo-ee-bay)	Into the third angle
Drun	(Dah-roo-noo)	Title of letter

E

E	(Ay)	I
Eca	(Ay-kah)	Therefore
Ecron	(Ay-kah-roh-noo)	Praise
Ed-nas	(Ay-dah Nah-ess)	Receivers
Ef	(Ay-eff)	Visit us
Efafage	(Ay-fah-fah-gay)	Vials
El	(Ay-lah)	The same
Elzap	(Ay-lah-zoad-ah-pay)	Course
Em	(Ay-mee)	Nine
Emod	(Ay-moh-dah)	8, 7, 6, 3

Emetgis	(Ay-may-tay-gees)	Seal
Emna	(Ay-mee-nah)	Herein
Enay	(Ay-nah-ee)	The Lord
Eors	(Ay-oh-ray-ess)	Thousand
Eran	(Ay-rah-noo)	6332 (6322)
Erm	(Ay-ray-mee)	Ark
Es	(Ay-ess)	Fourth
Esiasch	(Ay-see-ar-ess-cha)	Brothers
Ethamz	(Ay-tay-hah-me-zoad)	Are covered
Etharzi	(Ay-tay-hah-ray-zoad-ee)	Peace

F

F (also EF)	(Eff)	Visit
Fa-a-ip	(Fah ah ee-pay)	Your voices
Faboan	(Fah-boh-ah-noo)	Poison
Fafeh	(Fah-fay-hay)	Intent
Fafen	(Fah-fay-noo)	Your train
Fam	(Fah-mee)	Title of S
Faod	(Fah-oh-dah)	The Beginning
Faonts	(Fah-oh-nu-tay-ess)	Dwelling (verb)
Faorgt	(Fah-ohr-gee-tay)	Dwelling place
Fargt	(Fah-ray-gee-tay)	Their dwelling places
Farmz	(Fah-ray-mee-zoad)	Ye lifted up your voices
Faxs	(Fahx-ess)	7336
Fifalz	(Fee-fah-lah-zoad)	Weed out
Fifis	(Fee-fee-ess)	Execute

G

G	(Gee)	(With)
GA	(Gah)	31
Gah	(Gah-hay)	Spirits
Gal	(Gah-lah)	Title of D
G-chis-ge	(Gee Kah-hee-ess gay)	Are not the
Ge	(Gee)	Is not
Ged	(Gay-dah)	Title of G
Ge-Iad	(Gay Ee-ah-dah)	Our Lord and Master
Geobofal	(Gay-oh-bah-fah-lah)	Great Work
Ger	(Gay-ray)	Title of Q

Gigipah	(Gee-gee-pah-hay)	Living Breath
Gisa	(Gee-sah)	Title of T
Givi	(Gee-vee)	Stronger
Gizyaz	(Gee-zoad-ee-ah-zoad)	Mighty Earthquakes
Gnay	(Gee-nah-ee)	Doth
Gnetaab	(Gee-nay-tah-ah-bay)	Your Governments
Gnonp	(Gee-noh-nu-pay)	I garnished
Gohe (or Goho)	(Goh-hay)	Saith
Gohia	(Goh-hee-ah)	We say
Gohol	(Goh-hoh-el)	Saying
Goholor	(Goh-hoh-lohr)	Lift up
Gohulim	(Goh-hoo-leem)	It is said
Gohus	(Goh-hoos)	I say
Gon	(Goh-noo)	Title of I
Gono	(Goh-noh)	Faith
Gosao	(Goh-sah-oh)	Stranger
Graa	(Gee-rah-ah)	Moon
Graa	(Gee-rah-ah)	Marquises
Graph	(Gee-rah-pay-hay)	Title of E
Grosb	(Gee-roh-ess-bay)	Bitter Sting

H

Hami	(Hah-mee)	Creatures
Harg	(Hah-ray-gee)	Hath planted
Hoath	(Hoh-ah-tay-hay)	True Worshipper
Holdo	(Hoh-lah-doh)	Groaned aloud
Hol-q	(Hoh-lah Koh)	Measureth (ed)
Hom	(Hoh-mee)	Liveth
Homil	(Hoh-mee-el)	True Ages
Homin	(Hoh-mee-noo)	Age
Hubai	(Hoo-bah-ee)	Lanterns
Hubar	(Hoo-bah-ray)	Ever burning lamps
Hubard	(Hoo-bah-ray-dah)	Living lamps

I

I	(Ee)	Is
Iad	(Ee-ah-dah)	God
Iadnah	(Ee-ah-dah-nah-hay)	Knowledge

Iadnamad	(Ee-ah-dah-nah-mah-dah)	The undefiled knowledge
Iadpil	(Ee-ah-dah-pee-el)	Him
Iaiadix	(Ee-ah-ee-ah-deex)	Honour
Ia-ial	(Ee-ah ee-ah-el)	Conclude us
Iaida	(Ee-ah-ee-dah)	The highest, most high
Iaidon	(Ee-ah-ee-doh-noo)	All-powerful
Ial	(Ee-ah-el)	Burning
Ialpirgah	(Ee-ah-el-pee-ray-gah)	Flames of first glory
Ialpon	(Ee-ah-el-poh-noo)	Burn
Ialpor	(Ee-ah-el-poh-ray)	Flaming
Iaod (of)	(Ee-ah-oh-dah)	Beginning
Iarry	(Ee-oh-ray-ree)	Providence
ICH	(Ee-kah-hay)	11th Aethyr
Id	(Ee-dah)	Always
Idoigo	(Ee-doh-ee-goh)	Him that Sitteth on the Holy Throne
Ieh	(Ee-ay-hay)	Art
Iehusoz	(Ee-ay-hoo-soh-zoad)	His mercies
Iisonon	(Ee-ee-soh-noh-noo)	Branches
Ils	(Ee-el-ess)	O Thou
Ilsi	(Ee-el-see)	Thee
Im-va-mar	(Ee-mee vah mah-ray)	Apply yourselves
Insi	(Ee-noo-see)	Walkest
Iod	(Ee-oh-dah)	Him
Ioiad	(Ee-oh-ee-oh-dah)	Him that liveth forever
Ip	(Ee-pay)	Not
Ipam	(Ee-pah-mee)	Beginningless
Ipamis	(Ee-pah-mees)	Endless
Ipuran	(Ee-poo-rah-noo)	Shall not see
Yolcam	(Ee-oh-ol-kah-mee)	Bring forth
Yolci	(Ee-oh-el-kee)	Bringeth forth
Yor	(Ee-oh-ray)	Roll
Yrpoil	(Ee-ar-poh-ee-lah)	Division
Irgil	(Ee-ar-gee-lah)	How many
Isro	(Ee-ess-roh)	Promise
Ixomaxip	(Ee-x-oh-mohx-ee-pay)	Let her be known
Iza-zaz	(Ee-zoad-ah zoad-ah-zoad)	Have framed within
Izizop	(Ee-zoad-ee-zoad-oh-pay)	From the highest vessels

L

L	(Lah)	The first
L (o) (a)	(Lah)	The first one
Laiad	(Lah-ee-ah-dah)	The Secrets of Truth
Lap	(Lah-pay)	For
Larag	(Lah-rah-gee)	Neither
Las	(Lah-ess)	Rich
LEA	(Lah-ay-ah)	16th Aethyr
Lel	(Lay-lah)	The same
Levithmong	(Levee-tha-mon-gee)	The Beasts of the Field
LIL	(Lee-lah)	1st Aethyr
Limlal	(Lee-em-lah-lah)	His Treasure
LIN	(Lee-noo)	22nd Aethyr
LIT	(Lee-tay)	5th Aethyr
LOE	(Loh-ay)	12th Aethyr
Loholo (Sobolo)	(Loh-hoh-loh)	Shineth
Lolcis	(Loh-lah-kee-ess)	Bucklers
Loncho	(Loh-nu-kah-hoh)	Fall
Lon-doh	(Loh-noo doh)	Kingdoms
Lonsa (Lonshi)	Loh-noo-sah)	Power
Lonsh	(Loh-noo-ess-hay)	In power exalted
Lonshin	(Loh-noo-ess-hee-noo)	Their powers
Lors-l-q	(Loh-ray-ess el koh)	Flowers
Lrasd	(El-rah-ess-doh)	To dispose
Lring	(El-ree-nu-gee)	To stir up
Lu	(Loo)	Not or nor
Lucal	(Loo-kah-lah)	The North
Luciftian	(Loo-kee-eff-tee-ah-nu)	Ornaments of brightness
Luciftias	(Loo-ku-eff-tee-ah-ess)	Brightness
Lu-ia-he	(Loo ee-ah hay)	A Song of Honour
Lulo	(Loo-loh)	Tartar of Wine
Lusd (an)	(Loo-ess-dah)	Feet
Lusda	(Loo-ess-dah)	Their feet
Lusdi	(Loo-ess-dee)	My feet

M

Maasi	(Mah-ah-see)	Laid up
Mad	(Mah-dah)	The same your God
Madrid	(Mah-dah-ree-dah)	Iniquities

Madriiax	(Mad-dah-ree-ee-ahx)	O Ye Heavens
Malpirgi	(Mah-lah-pee-ar-gee)	Fires of life & increase
Malprg	(Mah-lah-pee-ar-gee)	Through-thrusting fire (Or Fiery Darts)
Mals	(Mah-lah-ess)	Title of P
Manin	(Mah-nu-nu)	In the Mind
Ma-of-fas	(Mah ohff fahs)	Not to be measured
Mapm	(Mah-pay-mee)	9639
Marb	(Mah-ah-bay)	According
Matorb	(Mah-toh-ar-bay)	Echoing
MAZ	(Mah-zoad)	6th Aethyr
Med	(May-dah)	Title of O
Miam	(Mee-ah-mee)	Continuance
Mian	(Mee-ah-nu)	3663
Micalp	(Mee-kah-el-pay)	Mightier
Micalzo	(Mee-kah-el-zoad-oh)	In Power
Micaolz	(Mee-kah-oh-el-zoad)	Mighty
Micma	(Mee-kah-mah)	Behold
Miinoag	(Mee-ee-noh-ah-gee)	Corners
Mir	(Mee-ray)	A torrent
Mirc	(Mee-ar-kah)	Upon
(z)Mnad	(Mee-nah-dah)	Another
Molap	(Moh-lah-pay)	Men
Molvi	(Moh-lah-vee)	Surges
Mom	(Moh-mee)	Moss
Momao	(Moh-mah-oh)	The Crowns
Momar	(Moh-mah-ray)	Shall be crowned
Monasci	(Moh-nah-ess-kee)	The Great Name
Monons	(Moh-noh-noo-ess)	Heart
Mooab	(Moh-oh-ah-bah)	It repenteth me
Mospleh	(Moh-ess-pay-lay-hay)	The Horns
Moz	(Moh-zoad)	Joy

N

Na	(Nah)	Your
Na-hath	(Nah Hah-tay-hay)	Title of H
Nana-e-el	(Nah-nah ay ay-lah)	My Power
Nanba	(Nah-noo-bah)	Thorns
Napeai	(Nah-pah-ay-ee)	Oh you swords

Napta	(Nah-pay-tah)	Two edge swords
Nazarth	(Nah-zoad-ahth)	Pillars of gladness
Nazavabb	(Nah-zoad-ah-vah-bay-bay)	Hyacinthine Pillars
Nazps	(Nah-zoad-pay-ess)	Sword or Earls
Netaab	(Nay-tah-ah-bay)	Government
NI	(Nee)	28
NIA	(Nee-ah)	24th Aethyr
Nibm	(Nee-bah-mee)	Season
Nidali	(Nee-dah-lee)	Mighty Sounds
Niis	(Nee-ee-ess)	Come Ye
Niiso	(Nee-ee-soh)	Come Away
Noaln	(Noh-ah-lah-noo)	May (be)
Noan (Noas)	(Noh-ah-noo)	Ye are become
(i) Noar	(Noh-ah-ray)	Become
Noasmi	(Noh-ah-ess-mee)	Let them become
Nobloh	(Noh-bay-loh)	The Palms
Noco	(Noh-koh)	Servant
Nocod	(Noh-koh-dah)	Thy servants
Noib	(Noh-ee-bay)	Yea!
Nonig	(Noh-mee-gee)	Even
Nonca	(Noh-noo-kah)	Unto You
Nonci (f)	(Noh-noo-kee)	O You (ye)
Noncp	(Noh-noo-kah-pay)	For You
Noquodi	(Noh-koo-oh-dee)	Their Ministers
(c) Noquol	(Noh-koo-oh-lah)	O Ye Servants
Nor	(Noh-ray)	Sons
Noromi	(Noh-roh-mee)	O Ye Sons!
Nor-molap	(Noh-ray moh-lah-pay)	Sons of Men
Nor-quasahi	(Noh-ray koo-ah-sah-hee)	Ye Sons of pleasure
Norz	(Noh-ray-zoad)	Six
Nothoa	(Noh-tay-hoh-ah)	In the midst (?)

O

O	(Oh)	5
O	(Oh)	Be
Oado	(Oh-ah-doh)	Weave
Oadriax	(Oh-ah-dah-ree-ahx)	Lower Heavens
Oali	(Oh-ah-lee)	I have placed
Oanio	(Oh-ah-nee-oh)	Moment
OB	(Oh-bay)	28

Obelisong	(Oh-bah-lee-soh-noo-gee)	Pleasant deliverers
Obloc	(Oh-bay-loh-kah)	A Garland
Oboleh	(Oh-boh-lay-hay)	Your Garments
Obza	(Oh-bay-zoad-ah)	Half
Od	(Oh-dah)	And
Odo	(Oh-doh)	Open or Openest
Odzi	(Oh-dah-zoad-ee)	Beginning
Oe	(Oh-ay)	Sing (ing)
O-q	(Oh koh)	But
Ohio	(Oh-hee-oh)	Woe
Ohorela	(Oh-ho-ray-lah)	I made a Law, Dukes
Oi	(Oh-ee)	This (or that is)
Oiad	(Oh-ee-ah-dah)	Just or God
Oiap	(Oh-ee-ah-pay)	The same
OL	(Oh-lah)	24th part
Ol	(Oh-lah)	I made you (I have made)
Olani	(Oh-lah-nee)	Two Times
Ollor	(Oh-lah-loh-ray)	Man
(Ollora, Ollog)	(Oh-lah-loh-rah)	Same
Oln	(Oh-lah-noo)	Made
Olpirt	(Oh-lah-pee-ray-tay)	Light
Om	(Oh-mee)	Know or Understand
Omoas	(Oh-mah-ah-ess)	Their Names
Oma (p)	(Oh-mah)	Understanding
Omax	(Oh-mahx)	Knowest
Ooa	(Oh-oh-ah)	Their
Ooaona	(Oh-oh-ah-oh-nah)	Eyes, visible appearance
Ooge	(Oh-oh-gay)	Chamber
Op	(Oh-pay)	22
Oroch (a)	(Oh-roh-kah-hay)	Under you (beneath)
Orri	(Oh-ray-ree)	Barren Stone
Ors	(Oh-ray-ess)	(with darkness)
Orscor	(Oh-ray-ess-koh-ray)	Dryness
Orsca	(Oh-ray-ess-kah)	Building
Orsha (Orsba)	(Oh-ray-ess-hah)	Drunken
Orth	(Oh-ray-tha)	Title of F
Os	(Oh-ess)	Twelve
Othil	(Oh-tay-hee-lah)	I have set
Ovcho	(Oh-voh-kah-hoh)	Let it confound
Ovof	(Oh-voh-eff)	May be magnified
Ovoars	(Oh-voh-ah-ar-ess)	The Center

134

Ox	(Ohx)	26
Oxex	(Ohx-ayx)	Vomit out
Oxiayal	(Ohx-ee-ah-yahl)	Mighty Seat
OXO	(Ohx-oh)	15th Aethyr
Ozazm	(Oh-zoad-ah-zoad-mee)	Make me
Ozol	(Oh-zoad-oh-lah)	Their heads
Ozongon	(Oh-zoad-oh-nu-goh-nu)	Manifold Winds
Ozozma	(Oh-zoad-oh-zoad-mah)	And make us

P

P	(Pay)	8
Pa	(Pah)	Be
Pa-aox (t)	(Pah-ahx)	Remain
Paeb	(Pah-ay-bay)	An Oak
Page	(Pah-gay)	Rest
Paid	(Pah-ee-dah)	Always
Pal	(Pah-lah)	Title of X
Pambt	(Pah-mee-bay-tay)	Unto me
Panpir	(Pah-noo-pee-ray)	Pouring down
Paombd	(Pah-oh-mee-bay-dah)	Her members
Papnor	(Pah-pay-noh-ray)	This remembrance
Par	(Pah-ray)	In Them
Parach	(Pah-rah-kah-hay)	Equal
Paracleda	(Pah-rah-kah-lay-dah)	A wedding
Paradial	(Pah-rah-dee-ah-lah)	Living dwellings
Paradizod	(Pah-rah-dee-zoad-oh-dah)	Virgins
Parm	(Pah-ray-mee)	Run
Parmg	(Pah-ray-mee-gee)	Let it run
Pashs	(Pah-ess-hay-ess)	Children
Patralx	(Pah-tay-rah-layx)	Rock
PAZ	(Pah-zoad)	4th Aethyr
Pd	(Pah-dah)	Thirty-three
Pe	(Pay)	Title of B
PEOAL	(Peh-oh-ah-lay)	5, 9, 6, 3, 6
Pi	(Pee)	Places (Bed)
Piad	(Pee-ah-dah)	Your God
Pi-adph	(Pee ah-dah-pay-hay)	Depths of my Jaws
Piamo-l	(Pee-ah-moh-ell)	Righteousness
Piap	(Pee-ah-pay)	Balance
Pidiai	(Pee-dee-ah-ee)	Marble

Pii	(Pee-ee)	Bed (or She is a place)
Pilah	(Pee-lah)	Moreover
Pild	(Pee-lah-dah)	Continually
Pilzin	(Pee-lah-zoad-ee-nu)	Firmament of Waters
Pir	(Pee-ray)	Holy Ones
Piripsax	(Pee-ree-pay-sahx)	With the Heavens
Piripsol	(Pee-ree-pay-sohl)	The Heavens
Plapli	(Pay-lah-pay-lee)	Partakers
Plosi	(Pay-loh-see)	As many
Poamal	(Poh-ah-mah-lah)	Your Palace
Poilp	(Poh-ee-lah-pay)	Are divided
Pop	(Poh-pay)	19th Aethyr
Praf	(Pay-rah-eff)	Dwell
Prdzar	(Pay-ray-dah-zoad-ahr)	Diminish
Prg	(Pay-ray-gee)	Flames
Prge	(Pay-ray-gay)	With the Fire
Prgel	(Pay-ray-gay-lah)	Of Fire
Priaz (i)	(Pay-ree-ah-zoad)	Those
Prt	(Pay-ray-tay)	Flame
Pugo	(Poo-goh)	Unto
Pu-im	(Poo-eem)	Sharp sickles (Knights)

Q

Q	(Koh)	Or
Q (Cocasb)	(Koh)	Content of Time
Qaa	(Kah-ah)	Your Garments
Qaaon (s)	(Kah-ah-oh-noo)	In Your Creation
Qanis	(Kah-nee-ess)	Olives
Qting	(Koh-tee-noo-gee)	The Rotten
Quaal (Quaadah)	(Koo-ah-ah-lah)	The Creator
Quar	(Koo-ah-ray)	1636
Quasb	(Koo-ah-ess-bay)	Destroy
Quasahi	(Koo-ah-sahee)	Pleasure
Qui-i-n	(Koo-ee ee noo)	Wherein
Qurlst	(Koo-arel-ess-tay)	As an handmaid

R

R	(Ar)

Ra-as (y)	(Rah ah-ess)	The East
Raclir	(Rah-kah-lee-ray)	Weeping
Restel	(Ray-ess-tay-lah)	That you may praise Him
RII	(Ree-ee)	29th Aethyr
Rior	(Ree-or-rah)	Widow
Ripir	(Ree-pee-rah)	No place
Ripson	(Ree-pay-soh-noo)	Heaven
Rit	(Ree-tay)	Mercy
Rlodnr	(Ree-loh-dah-noo-ar)	Mercury
(Ror)	(Roh-ray)	Sun, Kings
Roxtan	(Rohx-tah-nu)	Wine
Rsam	(Rah-sah-em)	Admiration

S

S	(Ess)	Fourth
Sa	(Sah)	In
Saanir	(Sah-ah-nee-ray)	Parts
Salbrox	(Sah-lah-brohx)	Sulphur
Sald	(Sah-lah-dah)	Wonder
Salman	(Sah-lah-mah-nu)	A house
Samvelg	(Sahm-vay-lah-gee)	To the Righteous
Sapah	(Sah-pah)	Mighty Sounds
Sision	(See-see-oh-noo)	Temple
Siatris	(See-ah-tay-ree-ess)	Scorpions
Sibsi	(See-bay-see)	The Covenant
So	(Soh)	In
Sobam	(Soh-bah-mee)	Whom
Sobha	(Soh-bay-hah)	Whose
Sobra	(Soh-bay-rah)	In whose
Solpeth	(Soh-lah-pay-tay-hay)	Hearken
Sonuf	(Soh-noof)	Reign
Surzas	(Soo-ray-zoad-ah-ess)	He hath sworn
Symp	(See-mee-pay)	Another

T

T	(Tay)	Also
Ta	(Tah)	As
Taba	(Tah-bah)	To Govern

Tabaame	(Tah-bah-ah-may)	Prelates (governors)
Tabaan	(Tah-bah-ah-nu)	Governor
Tabaord	(Tah-bah-oh-ray-dah)	Let her be governed
Tabaori	(Tah-bah-oh-ree)	Govern
Tabges	(Tah-bay-gay-ess)	Caves
Tal	(Tah-lah)	Title of M
Talbo	(Tah-lah-boh)	Cups
TAN	(Tah-noo)	17th Aethyr
Tastax	(Tah-ess-tayx)	Going Before
Tatan	(Tah-tah-noo)	Wormwood
Teloah	(Tay-loh-ah)	Death
Teloc (Vovim)	(Tay-loh-kah)	Him that is fallen
Teloch	(Tay-loh-kah-hay)	Death
TEX	(Tayx)	30th Aethyr
Thild	(Tay-hee-lah-dah)	Their own Seats
Thil (n)	(Tay-hee-lah)	Seats
Ti	(Tee)	It
Tia	(Tee-ah)	Unto us
Tianti	(Tee-ah-nu-tee)	She is (or bed)
Tibibf	(Tee-bee-bay-eff)	Sorrow
Tilb	(Tee-lah-bay)	Her
Tiobl	(Tee-oh-bay-lah)	In her
Tliob	(Tay-lee-oh-bay)	Separate, to
Toatar	(Toh-ah-tay-ray)	Hearken
Toh	(Toh-hay)	Triumpheth
Toglo	(Toh-gee-loh)	All things
Toibl	(Toh-ee-bay-lah)	Within her
Tonug	(Toh-nu-gee)	Let them be defaced
Tooart	(Toh-oh-oh-ray-tay)	Furnishing
TOR	(Toh-ray)	23rd Aethyr
Torg (i)	(Toh-ray-gee)	Creatures of Earth
Torzu	(Tor-zoad-oo)	Arise
Torzul	(Toh-ray-zoad-oo-lah)	Shall Rise
Torzulp	(Toh-ray-zoad-oo-lah-pay)	Rose Up
Tox	(Tohx)	Of Him
Tranan	(Tay-rah-noh-noo)	Marrow
Trian	(Tay-ray-ee-ah-nu)	Shall Be
Trint	(Tay-ray-ee-nu-tay)	Sit
Trof	(Tay-roh-eff)	Building
Turbs	(Toor-bay-ess)	Their Beauty

138

V

Vabzir	(Vah-bay-zoad-ee-ray)	Eagle
Vaoan	(Vay-oh-ah-noo)	Truth (purified, glorified)
Vau	(Vah-oo)	Title of U or V
Vaul	(Vah-oo-lah)	Work
Vaun	(Vah-oo-nu)	Ye might work
Vcim	(Vah-kah-ee-mee)	They frown not
Veh	(Vay-hay)	Title of C or K
Vap	(Vay-pay)	Flame
Vgear	(Vah-gay-ah-ray)	The strength of man
Vgeg (i)	(Vah-gay-gee)	Wax Strong
Vi	(Vee)	In
Vi-i-v	(Vee-ee-vah)	The second angle
Vin	(Vee-noo)	Invoke
Virq	(Vee-ray-koh)	Nests
Vi-v	(Vee vah)	The Second
Vlcinin	(Vah-lah-kee-nee-nu)	Happy is He
Vls	(Vah-lah-ess)	The Ends
V-ma-dea	(Vah-mah-day-ah)	Strong Towers
Vmd	(Vah-mee-dah)	Called
Vml	(Vah-mee-lah)	Add
Vmplif	(Vah-mee-pay-lee-eff)	Our Strength
Vnalah	(Vah-nah-lah)	Skirts
Vnas (Vnal)	(Vah-nah-ess)	These
Vnchi	(Vah-noo-kah-hee)	Confound
Vnd-l	(Vah-noo-dah-lah)	The rest
Vnig	(Vah-nee-gee)	Requireth
Vniglag	(Vah-nee-gee-lah-gee)	Descend
Vnph	(Von-pay-hay)	Anger
Vohim	(Voh-hee-mee)	Hundred
Vonpho	(Von-pay-hoh)	Wrath
Vonsarg	(Voh-nu-sah-ray-gee)	Everyone
Vooan	(Voo-ah-nu)	Truth, with them that fall
Vorsg	(Vor-sah-gee)	Over You
Vovina	(Voh-vee-nah)	The Dragon
Vp	(Vah-pay)	Not
V-pa-ah (i)	(Vah pay ah-hay)	Wings
Vran	(Vah-rah-noo)	The Elders
Vrbs	(Vah-ray-bay-ess)	Beautified
Vrelp	(Vah-ray-lah-pay)	A Strong Seer of Things

VTA	(Vah-tah)	14th Aethyr
VTI	(Vah-tee)	25th Aethyr
VX	(Vah-ex)	42
Un	(Oo-noo)	Title of A
Ur	(Oo-ray)	Title of L
Uran	(Oo-rah-noo)	Shall see

Z

Z (od)	(Zoad)	They (as)
ZAA	(Zoad-ah-ah)	27th Aethyr
Zacar-e	(Zoad-ah-kah-ray)	Move
Zamran	(Zoad-ah-mer-rah-noo)	Show Yourselves
Zar	(Zoad-ah-ray)	(Courses)
ZEN	(Zoad-ay-noo)	18th Aethyr
ZID	(Zoad-ee-dah)	8th Aethyr
Zien	(Zoad-ee-ay-nu)	My hands
Zildar	(Zoad-ee-lah-dah-ray)	Flew
Zilodarp	(Zoad-ee-loh-dah-ray-pay)	Conquest
ZIM	(Zoad-ee-mee)	13th Aethyr
Zimii	(Zoad-ee-mee-ee)	Have entered
Zimz (a)	(Zoad-ee-mee-zoad)	My vestures
ZIP	(Zoad-ee-pay)	9th Aethyr
Zir	(Zoad-ee-ray)	I am
Zirdo	(Zoad-ee-ray-doh)	I am
Zirn	(Zoad-ee-ray-noo)	Wonders
Zirom	(Zoad-ee-roh-mee)	There were
Zirop	(Zoad-ee-roh-pay)	Was
Zixlay	(Zoad-ix-lay)	To stir up
Zizop	(Zoad-ee-zoad-oh-pay)	Vessels
Zilda	(Zoad-lee-dah)	To water
Znrza	(Zoad-nu-ray-zoad-ah)	Sware
Z-ol	(Zoad oh-lah)	Hands
ZOM	(Zoad-oh-mee)	3rd Aethyr
Zomd	(Zoad-oh-mee-dah)	In the midst of
Zonac	(Zoad-oh-nah-kah)	They are apparelled
Zongon	(Zoad-oh-nu-goh-nu)	The Winds
Zonrensg	(Zoad-on-raynu-ess-gee)	Delivered
Zorge	(Zoad-or-gee)	Be friendly unto me
Zumbi	(Zoad-oo-mee-bee)	Seas
Zylna	(Zoad-ee-lah-nah)	In itself

Chapter Nine

The Lesser Ritual of the Hexagram

This ritual operates upon the Macrocosm in the same manner that the Pentagram ritual operates upon the Microcosm. It is to be performed after the "Lesser Ritual of the Pentagram" and is most appropriate for invocations of the Enochian Seniors.

1. Stand upright, feet together, left arm at side, right arm across body, holding the wand or other weapon upright in the median line. Then face East, and say:

2. "I.N.R.I.
Yod. Nun. Resh. Yod.
Virgo, Isis, Mighty Mother.
Scorpio, Apophis, Destroyer.
Sol, Osiris, Slain and Risen.
Isis, Apophis, Osiris, IAO."

3. Extend the arms in the form of a cross, and say:
"The sign of Osiris Slain." (See illustration.)

4. Raise the right arm to point upwards, keeping the elbow square, and lower the left arm to point downwards, keeping the elbow square, while turning the head over the left shoulder looking down so that the eyes follow the left forearm, and say:
"The sign of the Mourning of Isis" (See illustration.)

5. Raise the arms at an angle of sixty degrees to each other above the head, which is thrown back, and say:

"The sign of Apophis and Typhon." (See illustration.)

6. Cross the arms on the breast, and bow the head, and say: The sign of Osiris Risen." (See illustration.)

7. Extend the arms again as in (3) and cross them again as in (6), saying:
"L.V.X. Lux, the Light of the Cross."

8. With the magical weapon trace the Hexagram of Fire in the East, saying: "ARARITA."

(This is a word created by the initials of a Hebrew sentence which means "One is His Beginning: One is His Individuality: His Permutation is One.") This hexagram consists of two equilateral triangles, both apices pointing upwards. Begin at the top of the upper triangle and trace it in a clockwise direction. The top of the lower triangle should coincide with the central point of the upper triangle.

9. Turn to the South. Trace the Hexagram of Earth saying: "ARARITA."

This Hexagram has the apex of the lower triangle pointing downwards, and it should be capable of inscription in a circle.

10. Turn to the West. Trace the Hexagram of Air saying: "ARARITA."

This hexagram is like that of Earth: but the bases of the triangles coincide, forming a diamond.

11. Turn to the North. Trace the Hexagram of Water saying: "ARARITA."

This hexagram has the lower triangle placed above the upper, so that their apices coincide.

12. Return to the East and repeat steps (1—7)

The Banishing Ritual is identical, save that the direction of the Hexagrams must be reversed.

To invoke or banish Planets or Zodiacal signs, the Hexagram of Earth alone is used. Draw the hexagram, beginning from the point which is attributed to the planet your are dealing with.

Appendix

**The Corrected Holy Table
Diagram A**

Planetary Talismans
Diagram B

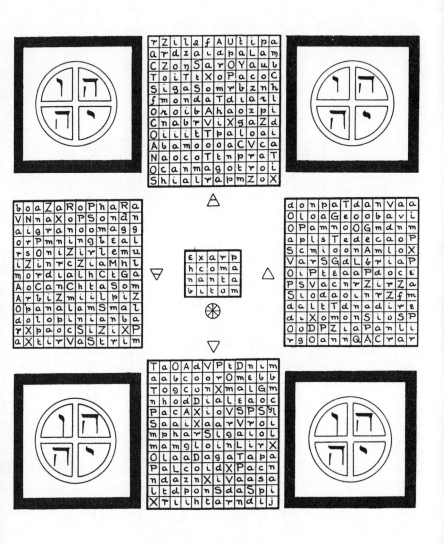

**The Elemental Tablets And Cherubic Emblems
Diagram C**

The Tablet Of Water
Great Central Cross And Subangles
Diagram D

**Four Elemental Tablets With Alternate Spellings
Diagram E**

The Sigils Of The Governors
Diagram F

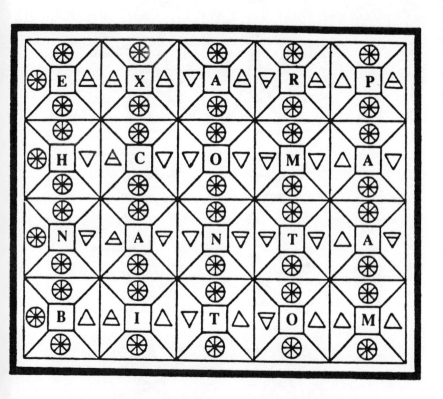

The Tablet Of Union (English Letters)
Diagram G

Pentagrams
Diagram H

Signs Of The Grades
Diagram I

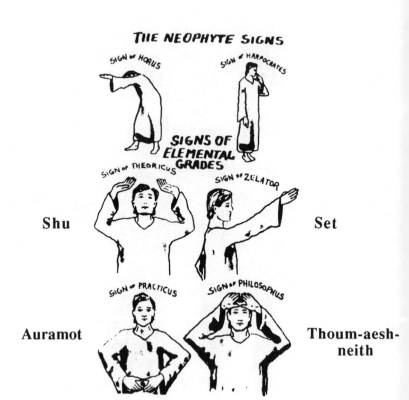

Shu

Set

Auramot

Thoum-aesh-neith

Diagram I

154

Sex Magick Symbols

**The Lovers
Divine And Elemental**

Babalon And The Beast Conjoined

The Quintessence Of Sexual Alchemy

**The Charging Of The Seed
Through Concentrated Will**

**The Holy Graal
The Creation Of The Elixir Of Life**

**The Annihilation Of The Ego
In The Thunder Orgasm**

**The Orgastic Circulation Of Light
The Supreme Attainment**

The Lingam And Yoni
Western Tantric Symbolism